BEYOND THE WHITE HOUSE

BEYOND THE WHITE HOUSE

WAGING PEACE, FIGHTING DISEASE, BUILDING HOPE

JIMMY CARTER

THORNDIKE PRESS

An imprint of Thomson Gale, a part of The Thomson Corporation

Detroit • New York • San Francisco • New Haven, Conn. • Waterville, Maine • London

THOMSON
™
GALE

LIBRARY OF CONGRESS CATALOGING-IN-PUBLICATION DATA

Carter, Jimmy, 1924–
    Beyond the White House : waging peace, fighting disease, building hope
/ Jimmy Carter. — Large print ed.
      p. cm. — (Thorndike Press large print nonfiction)
    Originally published: New York : Simon & Schuster, 2007.
    Includes index.
    ISBN-13: 978-1-4104-0270-7 (hardcover : alk. paper)
    ISBN-10: 1-4104-0270-3 (hardcover : alk. paper)
    1. Carter, Jimmy, 1924– 2. Carter, Jimmy, 1924– — Political and social
views. 3. Presidents — United States — Biography. 4. Presidents — Retirement — United States —Case studies. 5. Human rights workers —United
States — Biography. 6. Humanitarianism —Case studies. 7. Emory University. Carter Center. 8. Large type books. I. Title.
E873.A3 2007b
973.926092--dc22

                                                    2007035838

Published in 2007 in arrangement with Simon & Schuster, Inc.

Printed in the United States of America on permanent paper
10 9 8 7 6 5 4 3 2 1

*With appreciation to my dedicated partners
at The Carter Center*

Peace is more than just the absence of war.
People everywhere seek an inner peace
that comes from the right to voice their views,
choose their leaders, feed their families,
and raise healthy children.
— Jimmy Carter

CONTENTS

PREFACE

In a television interview on my seventieth birthday, Barbara Walters asked, "Mr. President, looking back on your time as a submarine officer, a farmer and businessman, as governor, and in Washington, what has been the best of all?" Not having been asked this question before, I thought before replying, "By far, my best years are those I'm enjoying now, since Rosalynn and I left the White House."

This is still true, not only because of our growing family and a relatively secluded private life when we are in Plains but also because of the excitement, challenge, unpredictability, adventure, and gratification of our Carter Center's work in more than seventy nations around the world.

Unlike those where I concentrated most of my attention during the presidential years, most of these nations do not play a major role in shaping the world's political, military, and economic future. Our most dedicated investments of time and energy have been among the poorest and most forgotten, the people of Guyana, East Timor, Haiti, Mali, Burkina Faso, Ethiopia, Niger, Liberia, Côte d'Ivoire, Mozambique, Nicaragua, Ghana, and in other communities in Africa, Latin America, and the Middle East.

Instead of Departments of State, Defense, and Commerce, we have a small group of associates at The Carter Center that includes some of the world's foremost experts on conflict prevention, human rights, mental health, agriculture, disease control and prevention, and promoting democracy. A superb group of student interns, so far representing almost 350 universities around the world, analyze complex political interrelationships and provide intelligence briefings that often excel what is furnished by the CIA.

Working closely with local governments and with many other organizations, we go directly to the villages and the homes of those who are in need. This intimate relationship with people we have not known before is an emotional and often a spiritual experience. Our natural human tendency is to underestimate those who are poor and cannot provide their families with basic necessities. We have learned that they are just as ambitious, hardworking, and intelligent, and their family values are as ours. They take full advantage of any opportunity to improve their lives.

This book is drawn from the personal diaries of Rosalynn's and my work with The Carter Center during the last twenty-five years. It has been a great pleasure for me to review these activities and to share some of them with you.

Jimmy Carter
July 2007

CHAPTER ONE
THE EARLY DAYS

It was just a week after the 1980 presidential election when the "blind" trustee of our estate, the attorney Charles Kirbo, called from Atlanta and asked to see me. He had become my lawyer when I successfully contested an election stolen from me in 1962, was a close adviser when I later ran for governor of Georgia, and served as chairman of the Democratic Party of Georgia. That day in November, Kirbo shared a cool drink with Rosalynn and me on the Truman Balcony of the White House and, after we'd exchanged some family information and a few jokes with a South Georgia flavor, he informed us that he had some good news and some bad news about our family's farm and warehouse business.

The good news was that our land was still there and the pine trees were growing. The bad news was that, after three years of drought and some mismanagement,

President Carter receives traditional Ghanaian attire, a gift from the chief of Tingoli village in northern Ghana. (PETER DiCAMPO)

Carter's Warehouse was a million dollars in debt. Because we had pledged to remove ourselves completely from any involvement in or knowledge of our personal investments or business affairs, this was the first financial accounting that Rosalynn and I had received since we moved to Washington. We were surprised and appalled. We had left a thriving farm-supply business, free of debt, and we'd assumed that it had continued to be a lucrative investment.

We returned home about two months later with two heavy financial burdens, the lesser of which was to pay our accumulated business debts. More burdensome by far was my obligation to select a site and build a presidential library that could house almost 27 million official documents and papers, plus millions of photographs, visual records, and other mementos accumulated during my administration. Always a poor fund-raiser and now a defeated candidate for reelection who had made no plans for this all-too-early eventuality, I dreaded the prospect of raising the necessary funds, which had to come from private contributions. The prolonged holding of our hostages by Iranian militants had not made me the most popular ex-president to survive his White House years.

In a somewhat naïve moment soon after Election Day, I had told the White House press corps that I intended to emulate President Harry Truman and refrain from using my service in office as a means of enriching myself. I had said, "There may be some kinds of benevolent or nonprofit corporations in which I will let my influence and my ability be used, but not in a profit-making way." At that time, I had no other plans to utilize my presidential experiences.

Rosalynn and I were able to sell what remained of our business, and I signed a contract to write my presidential memoir. We were able to salvage our home in Plains and our two tracts of land, one of which had been acquired by our ancestors in 1833 and the other, the "new farm," in 1904.

Working closely with me, Georgia Governor George Busbee had appointed a committee that recommended a place for the presidential library. We ultimately selected a beautiful thirty-acre site about halfway between Atlanta's downtown business area and Emory University. It commanded a good view of the city, having been the headquarters of Union General William Tecumseh Sherman, who had stood on one of the site's hilltops in 1864 to watch Atlanta burn.

During the next year, I used the five thousand pages of diary notes I had dictated during my administration to complete *Keeping Faith,* and I spent most of my other time seeking contributions for the library. It became increasingly obvious that we needed a more attractive reason for potential contributors than just "to store our White House records." This need converged with another question that confronted us: What would we do with the rest of our lives? At the age of fifty-six, I was the youngest presidential survivor since William Howard Taft. I had a statistical life expectancy of twenty-five more years. I pondered this question, apparently even subconsciously.

Although I am generally a sound sleeper, I awoke one night and sat up in bed, surprising Rosalynn. She asked, "What's the matter, Jimmy? Are you ill or did you have a nightmare?"

I replied, "No, but I've just had a thought about what we can do in addition to building the presidential library. We can start an adjacent institution, something like Camp David, where people can come who are involved in a war. I can offer to serve as a mediator, in Atlanta or perhaps in their countries. We might also study and teach how to resolve or prevent conflict." This was the birth of what was to be The Carter Center.

I received several offers in the academic world, including two inquiries about positions as president of universities. Having had enough of politics and already burdened down with fund-raising obligations, I declined. From within Georgia, however, came three attractive offers to assume the role of distinguished professor. One was from the Georgia Board of Regents, to lecture in the thirty-three colleges and universities in the state system; the others came from Mercer University and from Dr. James Laney, president of Emory University. Laney assured me that I would have a chance during each year to lecture in all the schools of the university and that my comments would never be restricted or censored in any way. I chose Emory and announced this decision in April 1982, along with plans to establish an institute that might be associated with the university.

With Dr. Steven Hochman as my assistant, we established an office for our Center on the top floor of the Emory University library and soon expanded the focus of our work to a broad range of issues, still including conflict resolution, especially in the Middle East, but also human rights, nuclear arms control, global health, and the environment, with a special emphasis on Latin America.

The Carter Center is headquartered in Atlanta, Georgia. Led by Jimmy and Rosalynn Carter, Center staff have worked in more than seventy nations to wage peace, fight disease, and build hope for some of the world's most forgotten people. (THE GEORGIA HIGH PROGRAM)

In 1984 we began construction of the Presidential Library and Museum, and The Carter Center, partly with borrowed money, and the facilities were dedicated two years later, on October 1 (my birthday), with a speech by President Ronald Reagan. The library and records were delivered for permanent ownership and operation to the U.S. National Archives and Records Administration. On the other side of two small lakes were the circular buildings that would house The Carter Center.

The Center staff had moved in by the time of the dedication. The library and museum opened on the same day, and the files housed in the Presidential Library were made available to researchers in January 1987. My instructions have always been to expedite the availability of the classified documents, though this process has been subverted by an increasing preoccupation in Washington with tight and unnecessary secrecy. Despite this official impediment, we developed a harmonious relationship between The Carter Center and the National Archives. We have shared responsibility for the exterior grounds and parking areas, as well as an agreement that no substantive changes can be made in the museum exhibits without my approval, and professional archivists have exclusive control over the written and visual records of my political career.

BASIC PRINCIPLES

As we expanded our first concept for The Carter Center, a set of seven principles emerged:

1. We would not duplicate or compete with effective work being done by others, such as United Nations agencies, the U.S. government, other nongovernmental organizations, think tanks, or universities. Instead we would fill vacuums in addressing issues that were important to our country or to other people.
2. Ours would not be a partisan approach. Whenever possible, we would recruit prominent Republicans or foreign leaders to share the responsibilities of leadership.
3. The Carter Center would be an action agency, not just devoted to theoretical or academic analysis of issues. We would convene other institutions to foster cooperation, and our conferences would include knowledgeable experts on the adopted subject, but the presumption was for us to be directly

involved in implementing the ideas and recommendations.

4. We would not permit the prospect of potential failure to deter us from making our best effort but would be willing to take chances if the goals were worthy.

5. As a personal restraint, I would not intrude into a politically sensitive area without first obtaining at least tacit permission from the White House.

6. In certain projects, we would utilize a generic name, "Global 2000," instead of "Carter Center" or my name. This would permit village chiefs or heads of state to feel a genuine sense of partnership and be able to claim credit when successes were realized.

7. I would prepare detailed trip reports on my way home from foreign visits and share them immediately with my family, our staff members, and key supporters of our Center. I would also send slightly edited copies to leaders in the White House, the State Department, and the United Nations. [Reports are also posted on our website, www.cartercenter.org.]

Almost uniquely, The Carter Center would

be fulfilling the role of think tank but be primarily an action agency dedicated to achieving specific goals. We visited a number of universities and other institutes as the Center was being established, to assess their programs and to learn from their experiences. There were many warnings about any binding relationships with other organizations that might infringe on our independence or conflict philosophically or politically with our purposes. One notable example of incompatibility had been policy conflicts between the relatively liberal Stanford University and the adjacent Hoover Institution, which was known for its conservative orientation.

We were fortunate to have the advice of Warren Christopher, who served as deputy secretary of state in my administration and was then chairman of the Stanford University trustees. His group of distinguished advisers proposed a framework that would let our Center work in harmony with Emory University. Representatives of the Center and Emory reached an agreement in 1994, after five years of consultation. The Center would retain its permanent independence and be governed by a board of trustees on which Rosalynn and I would serve as chairpersons. Half of the remaining trustees would be selected by us and approved by the Emory trustees, and the other half, including Emory's president, would be selected by the university and approved by us, for a total of about two dozen.

One of the Emory committees struggled with how to express the prospect of a future without Rosalynn or me, sometimes with peals of laughter at their efforts to be sensitive to our feelings about prospective death. I finally wrote a poem about the quandary:

Committee of Scholars Describe the Future Without Me

Some shy professors, forced to write
about a time that's bound to come
when my earthly life is done
described my demise
in lovely euphemistic words
invoking pleasant visions of
burial rites, with undertakers,
friends, and pious pastors
gathered round my flowered casket
eyes uplifted
breaking new semantic ground
not by saying
I have passed on
joined my Maker
or gone to the promised land

but stating the lamented fact
in the best of terms
that I, now dead, have
reduced my level of participation.

Both before and after my level of participation would be reduced, The Carter Center would raise its own funds and employ its own people, but we would comply with the university's personnel policies, and any of our income above that needed for annual budgets would be invested by the university along with its own endowment. Leaders in charge of our programs, called fellows, could also serve as professors at the university when desirable. I am beginning my twenty-sixth year as University Distinguished Professor, and Rosalynn also continues as a University Fellow.

In the midst of struggling to raise enough donations to finance our programs and to retire our construction debt, I was appalled when Christopher's group recommended that we also raise an endowment of $12 million. I could see myself spending the rest of my life raising funds, but I reluctantly agreed. Over the years, this goal has increased to $25 million, $100 million, and ultimately $250 million, which we have now exceeded. This, along with our partnership with Emory and the development of a world-wide array of leaders and financial supporters who cooperate with us in our multiple programs, is one of the guarantees that The Carter Center will be a permanent institution.

At the beginning, I established some conservative fiscal policies for The Carter Center that have been strictly observed. Although we had to borrow several million dollars to complete our original buildings, furnishings, and grounds, we repaid these debts as quickly as possible and, since then, have maintained a balanced budget. We have refrained from launching even our most desired projects until funding was assured, a policy that requires the development of proposals adequately specific and attractive to warrant the support of sometimes doubting prospective donors. Since the basic character and purpose of our Center were unprecedented, we had to prove the worth of our efforts step by step, accumulating new and expanded financial sources as we demonstrated tangible results.

I have always spent a lot of time visiting prospective donors, both in the United States and abroad. Our country is blessed with large benevolent foundations, and some of them gave us strong support even before we had a proven record of achievement. Those established by the families of Ford, Rockefeller, Carnegie, Starr, Hewlett, Packard, MacArthur, and Woodruff were especially helpful. Canada and some of the European governments seemed to be looking for programs to support that would enhance peace, freedom, democracy, human rights, environmental quality, and the alleviation of suffering, and they became permanent partners with The Carter Center. I also found strong support in Japan, from both semiprivate and government sources. The Bill & Melinda Gates Foundation has become the largest donor of all, and their special interest in tropical diseases has made them a natural partner.

Although we never permitted the offer of funding to shape our agenda, there were times when the special desire of a donor was compatible with our own priorities. The Hilton Foundation and Lions Clubs International had special interests in combating diseases that cause blindness, and they have given us strong and sustained support in our dealing with onchocerciasis (river blindness) and trachoma. The Sasakawa Foundation in Japan provided funding for increasing the yield of food grains in Africa.

During recent years we have stabilized our

number of full-time employees at about 150, and our cash budgets at $35–$40 million. A quick calculation will reveal that this requires the raising of about $100,000 in cash contributions every day of the year.

We had some loyal supporters from my political years, and we soon initiated an effort to raise funds through exploratory direct mailings. The number of contributors from this source has grown to about 250,000, and they furnish about 15 percent of our total budgeted funds. I spend a day each month calling these unknown partners personally, to thank as many as possible and to invite them to visit our Center to learn more about us. Many of them who begin with donation of five dollars or so ultimately become major annual contributors. Several hundred of these donors come to Atlanta for a full day each year to learn about our programs, and about two-thirds of them spend an extra day in Plains with Rosalynn and me — to learn about our hometown, to join in a square dance on the city street, and to attend my Bible class on Sunday morning.

One of my most gratifying surprises has been the generosity of major corporations, especially in providing their own products for benevolent causes. When I have gone to the corporate headquarters or made other appeals to DuPont, Merck, GlaxoSmith-Kline, Pfizer, or American Cyanamid (now BASF), they have contributed many millions of dollars' worth of filter cloths, medicines, and pesticides. Although it is difficult to put an exact price on these contributions, their total value is several times larger than our cash budgets.

Rosalynn and I have attempted to help The Carter Center financially with personal contributions, from the Nobel and other awards, and income from my speeches and some of the books I have written. Another opportunity developed when we began to have our "Winter Weekends," when about three hundred of our donors join us and pay a fee that covers the cost of transportation, room and board, ski lessons, and other entertainment. The highlight of each event and most of our profit comes on our final night, with an auction of contributed items. Delta Air Lines always donates a number of trips to exotic vacation spots, manufacturers have given us automobiles, owners of yachts have loaned them for weeklong cruises, stream owners have permitted weekends of fly-fishing for trout, and other friends have made a wide range of interesting gifts.

As a lifetime woodworker and an amateur

artist and winemaker, I have crafted furniture, provided originals or copies of my oil paintings, and donated bottles of white and red wine. The crafted pieces have included hand tools, a duck decoy, cedar chests, end tables, hand-carved chess sets, bookcases, cabinets, sets of stools, a four-poster bed, and a baby cradle. I have enjoyed selecting special woods for these items, including green wood from hickory trees behind our home, walnut from our mountain cabin in North Georgia, paulownia (a very fast-growing tree) that I have planted on our farm, a persimmon tree that lay underwater in a Georgia stream for more than 150 years, and a special cherry tree that developed a rare tiger-striped interior.

Another popular offering has been photographs taken at the dedications of presidential libraries. There were five presidents at the new Reagan library, and I suggested that all of us and the first ladies sign a very limited number of photographs and then divide them equally among us. Richard Nixon, Gerald Ford, Ronald Reagan, George H. W. Bush, and I all agreed, as did our wives and Lady Bird Johnson. We also pledged not to sign any other copies in the future. These autographed photographs are some of the most attractive presidential mementos for collectors and have sometimes competed with my furniture for the highest prices at our auctions.

We now have net proceeds of more than a million dollars from each of the weekends, but the most valuable benefit is that each year these gatherings attract a new group of potential supporters, many of whom become permanent partners.

Although I managed most of the Center's affairs during the first few years, it became obvious after we completed our new facilities that an experienced leader was needed to work full-time. Dr. William Foege, former director of the Centers for Disease Control and Prevention, joined The Carter Center in 1986 as its executive director and coordinator of our developing health projects. While I was president, Rosalynn had promoted a greatly expanded program of child immunization in America, and under Bill Foege's guidance and inspiration our Center became involved in a similar effort on a worldwide basis. This would soon lead us to adopt specific programs in fighting disease and promoting nutrition, primarily in Africa. Bill remains a trusted adviser; he was succeeded in 1992 by Dr. John Hardman as executive director.

CHAPTER TWO
WAGING PEACE

MIDDLE EAST PEACE

The first project that The Carter Center adopted was to assess prospects for peace between Israel and its neighbors. The Reagan administration had not shown any real interest in implementing the terms of the Camp David peace agreements that I had negotiated in 1978 and 1979, and we felt free to address the issue. Following a visit to the Middle East in March 1983, and working closely with Emory professor Kenneth Stein and former associates from my presidency, we invited a wide range of interested persons, including top leaders from Saudi Arabia, Lebanon, Egypt, Syria, Jordan, Israel, the Palestinian community, and current representatives of the U.S. government, to participate. When each delegation arrived in Atlanta, they were welcomed and hosted throughout the conference by a small group of students from Emory who had been thoroughly briefed about the special interests of the assigned group.

President Gerald Ford joined us in presiding over the discussions, which were remarkably frank and often controversial. All the participants gained a renewed appreciation for the complexity of the issues, and also some insight into what steps might be taken in the future. Following our conferences, the different groups of Emory students had their own conference. Jerry Ford and I went to Washington, where we gave briefings to key congressional leaders and representatives of the administration. Our primary goal was to reinvigorate the dormant peace process.

The consultation process also resulted in 1985 in a book, *The Blood of Abraham,* in which I described the overall situation with unedited assessments from the perspectives of leaders with whom I had long talks in Israel, the occupied Palestinian territories, Syria, Jordan, Egypt, and Lebanon. Sometimes I was provided a confidential agenda by national security advisers or from the U.S. State Department to explore with leaders; at other times, Rosalynn and Dr. Stein would participate in the meetings. Invariably, I made a written or personal report to the White House and State Department, and usually to the secretary-general of the

United Nations, on the results.

We saw enough interest and desire for a renewed peace effort to organize another session at The Carter Center in November 1987. This time, our co-chairs were the *Foreign Affairs* editor William Hyland and Under Secretary-General of the United Nations Brian Urquhart. We made a special effort to have strong representatives from all the permanent members of the UN Security Council, and I made a trip to explain to leaders in China, the Soviet Union, France, and Great Britain the purposes of our conference and to ensure that they would cooperate. The parties in the Middle East were also represented, with Palestinian spokesmen included in the Jordanian delegation, and we also had participants from the academic world. (We were precluded by U.S. government policy from dealing directly with the Palestine Liberation Organization.) Members of the UN Security Council and U.S. State Department played a role in the deliberations.

Three unanimous recommendations emerged:

1. An international conference should lead to direct peace negotiations, based on UN Resolutions 242 and 338 and

also on the Framework for Peace promulgated by the Camp David Accords of 1978.

2. The conference should not impose a solution, nor should the participants be given the ability to veto agreements reached among the parties.

3. Palestinian participation should be assured, perhaps within the context of a Jordanian-Palestinian delegation.

Referring to our final report, the London *Financial Times* stated, "Four of the U.N.'s five permanent members wholeheartedly support it, while the fifth, the U.S., says it will back any process that will lead to direct negotiations." In fact, within a few months, U.S. Secretary of State George Shultz issued a very similar peace initiative, and President Ronald Reagan made a strong statement promoting implementation of the Camp David Accords, deploring the expansion of Israeli settlements in Palestinian territories, and encompassing the basic recommendations of our conference. I was grateful that the president asked me to help in drafting this speech but disappointed that no action was taken to convene direct peace talks.

Complying with our Center's general principles, we reduced our direct involvement in the Middle East when President George H. W. Bush and Secretary of State James Baker became more active in the region by bringing Palestinians and other involved parties together in 1991 at a conference in Madrid. Indirectly, this would lead to the Oslo peace agreement of 1993, which we monitored closely.

NUCLEAR ARMS CONTROL

In May 1984, President Gerald Ford agreed to join me in assessing the status of nuclear arms control. For our conference at Emory in 1985 we invited representatives from nations that acknowledged their possession of nuclear armaments. We were pleased that Soviet ambassador Anatoly Dobrynin brought the foremost military and civilian leaders from his country. Our primary goal was to understand and then publicize a current analysis of international agreements, the degree of compliance with them, and recommendations for additional action. We attempted to emphasize the substantial consensus that was evident, sent our report and recommendations to political leaders in both nuclear and nonnuclear nations, and promulgated a summary of our findings through the news media.

Former Georgia senator Sam Nunn and

others later established centers for the study of the nuclear arms issue, so in recent years we at The Carter Center have limited our efforts to the assembly every five years of the key participants who join in the Review Conference on the international Nuclear Non-Proliferation Treaty. Invariably, there are sharp differences between the United States, which wants to focus on selective objections to expansion of nuclear arsenals, and the large group of nations that are technologically capable of producing nuclear weapons but refrain from doing so and desire a serious commitment to nuclear disarmament by the existing nuclear powers. We continue to monitor closely both compliance with and violation of the Nuclear Non-Proliferation Treaty and other nuclear agreements, and strongly condemn the recent abandonment by the United States of those agreements previously negotiated and its failure to pursue other restraints.

SOVIET MEDIA

One of our early goals at The Carter Center was to promote democracy and freedom in the Soviet Union, and we adopted an intriguing partnership with Dr. Ellen Mickiewicz, who was a professor and dean of the graduate school at Emory University. As I visited the Emory campus for my lectures and monthly meetings with the university's president and key faculty members, I had noticed enormous antennae on top of two buildings, focused eastward and low above the horizon. I soon learned that they were controlled by Dr. Mickiewicz and, since 1984, had been aimed constantly at the satellite over the Soviet Union that transmitted First Program, the most important Soviet television network, where the only live news broadcasts were permitted. Dr. Mickiewicz and a small group of students and volunteers, all fluent in Russian, were monitoring the official programs of entertainment and propaganda of the Soviet government, viewed by almost 200 million people.

Whenever there was even a subtle change in the policy of the Soviet leaders, it could be detected earliest by careful observation of the daily news telecasts. This evolution was obviously of great interest and importance as leadership changed during the 1980s from Leonid Brezhnev to Yuri Andropov to Konstantin Chernenko to Mikhail Gorbachev. The Emory monitors' computer database encompassed a collection of Soviet television commentaries that permitted analysis of official policies regarding particular countries or subjects. I soon learned that neither the

CIA nor the State Department had this capability, and their representatives would often derive information from this monitoring program.

In 1986, Ellen Mickiewicz became our Center's Soviet media and international communications fellow. Our early purpose was to make a thorough assessment of media broadcasts to the Soviet people and to promote increased flexibility and freedom in television broadcasting. This effort would, of course, have to include an equal exchange of information and advice. Dr. Mickiewicz formed a working relationship with Soviet researchers to devise the framework for a scholarly exchange, and in a visit to Moscow I found that Mikhail Gorbachev was eager to promote this partnership. We quickly organized annual meetings to alternate between our Center and locations in the Soviet Union, including Moscow, St. Petersburg, and Alma-Ata, Kazakhstan. Subsequently, we increased our coverage to include radio broadcasts and added meeting sites in Eastern Europe.

Usual participants at these sessions would include top executives of the major American television networks, the chairman of the Federal Communications Commission, the chairman of the Soviet cable association, directors of the television systems, and media advisers to the Soviet president. We also invited experts and academics who specialized in the shaping of public opinion in the United States and the USSR. Detailed comparisons were made between the contents of the major television programs in our two countries.

These were exciting sessions, as the Soviet representatives became increasingly able to report progress in the diversity of their media, both by private ownership of some stations and in the number of programs permitted to be broadcast. There was an explosion of sources of programming under Gorbachev, with his glasnost and perestroika policies, and the number of competing transmitters soon grew into the hundreds. I recall that, in Lithuania alone, twenty-two television stations evolved. One of the problems that developed was pirating from American and other sources, as movies and entertainment programs were simply downloaded from satellite channels and rebroadcast.

For some years, foreign ownership of television channels was permitted in the Soviet Union and Russia, but this freedom has been curtailed under the more authoritarian and restrictive policies of Vladimir Putin. At least in a small way, The Carter Center's work with Dr. Mickiewicz helped to bring an element of freedom and democracy to the Soviet Union as it disintegrated into fifteen nations.

CONFLICT RESOLUTION

During 1984 we concentrated on expanding our peacemaking capabilities by recruiting Dr. Dayle Powell to be our fellow in conflict resolution and Dr. Robert Pastor to head our programs in this hemisphere. One of our most challenging and interesting events was held in 1985 at Callaway Gardens in West Georgia and was designed by Dr. Powell to illustrate the technique of mediation. The intransigent subject chosen was tobacco: its production, sale, use, and impact on health and the economy. We wanted to explore intense differences of opinion, so we invited farmers and commissioners of agriculture from tobacco-producing states, health experts who specialized in the ravages of tobacco, and foremost practitioners of mediation from Harvard, George Mason, and other universities. Although sharply divided and even antagonistic at first, the major participants finally reached a consensus. Tobacco producers were unanimous in not wanting their own children to smoke or to use snuff or chewing tobacco, and those interested in health agreed that some financial alternative was needed to sustain the income of farm families who would agree to stop producing the toxic weed.

We began to analyze all the conflicts in the world, using techniques that were mainly derived from Uppsala University in Sweden. At the time, there were thirty-four conflicts around the world defined as "major," each having had at least a thousand battle-related deaths. We assigned analysis of each of them to one or two interns, who collected up-to-date information from official documents and news media from the conflict area, along with statements by government officials and guerrilla leaders. I received a combined report each month and was surprised to learn that nearly all of these conflicts were civil wars, within the borders of the affected nations.

In 1987 we convened at The Carter Center the secretaries-general of the United Nations, the Organization of American States, and the Commonwealth of Nations to discuss the challenges and opportunities of dispute resolution. It was disheartening to learn that the charters of these organizations limited them to addressing conflicts between nations. As a result of this meeting, we formed the International Negotiation Network, including members such as Javier Pérez de Cuéllar (former secretary-general of the United Nations), Oscar Arias (former president of Costa Rica), Olusegun Obasanjo (former president of Nigeria), Cyrus Vance (former U.S. secretary of state), Eduard Shevardnadze (former Soviet foreign minister), Andrew Young (former U.S. ambassador to the United Nations), Shridath Ramphal (former secretary-general of the Commonwealth of Nations), Bishop Desmond Tutu of South Africa, Lisbet Palme (wife of the prime minister of Sweden), Marie-Angélique Savané of Senegal, and Elie Wiesel (Holocaust survivor). I served as chairman, and our group has exchanged advice and counsel over the years.

Although we were eager to serve as mediators or negotiators and received many requests to do so, we found that rarely would both sides to a conflict decide at the same time that they were ready to seek agreement. It was usually the losers who appealed to us, while those who were currently dominant felt that they could win militarily and didn't need assistance from outsiders.

This frequently occurring impasse ultimately led The Carter Center to seek to prevent conflict by monitoring elections. In our conversations with military leaders already at war or contemplating the resolution of a dispute by combat, we utilized a truism of politics. Each candidate is inclined to think, "If an honest election is held, surely the people will reject these other jokers and choose me — the most admirable and competent candidate." Our intent was to capitalize on this belief and convince both sides that we could help ensure a fair electoral contest. Our efforts to establish new democracies or to preserve old ones that are endangered have led us to monitor almost seventy elections around the world during the past eighteen years.

NORTH KOREA

The Carter Center involvement in North Korea was perhaps the most controversial and important of all its efforts. For almost four years, beginning in 1990, Kim Il Sung, the dictatorial communist leader of the Democratic People's Republic of Korea (DPRK), had requested that I find some way to visit Pyongyang. His contacts with me were usually his nation's representatives to the United Nations, and the U.S. government imposed a twenty-five-mile limit on their travel. Usually they made arrangements to meet me on my visits to New York,

46

and on two occasions they managed to gain approval to come to Georgia. Increasingly, their messages were focused on the growing crisis caused by the prospect of the DPRK's reprocessing of nuclear fuel rods removed from their antiquated power reactor, which used carbon as a moderator.

They knew of my background in nuclear reactor design from my Navy days and claimed that they wanted to avoid any confrontation with the United States and other concerned nations. The basic problem was that our country had outlawed all direct communications with the leaders of North Korea. President Bill Clinton was responding to this challenge by seeking UN Security Council approval of economic sanctions even more restrictive than those that had been in effect since the Korean War. With a vote in the United Nations pending, my concern was increased by some Chinese visitors who told me the result might very well be another war on the Korean peninsula. They said that the sanctions would be interpreted as an international condemnation of the North Korean government and a personal insult to North Korea's revered (almost worshipped) leader, and that the only response from the isolated and paranoid people would be to launch a massive attack on South Korea.

On June 1, 1994, I called President Clinton to express my concerns, and he said that he was leaving for Europe in a few hours but would send a senior official to Plains to brief me. Two days later I was informed that a junior member of the White House staff would give the briefing, but it would have to be postponed for a few days. I expressed my displeasure to the president's chief of staff, who promised me an immediate briefing from Ambassador Robert Gallucci, coordinator of an interagency group dealing with the Korean crisis.

Our Center's director of programs, former ambassador Marion Creekmore, joined me and Rosalynn at our home for an excellent three-hour presentation by Gallucci, who seemed to share our trepidation about Pyongyang's likely reaction to sanctions. He said that the president was committed to impose sanctions on the DPRK because they had not complied with commitments of the Non-Proliferation Treaty. There could be no communication with leaders in Pyongyang except intermittently through their UN ambassador, Ho Jung, and no real assurance about whether the messages were delivered. The entire situation was a comedy of errors, and the administration was divided on what should be done.

When Gallucci left, I began considering the consequences of going to North and South Korea just representing The Carter Center, with or without approval from Washington. In effect, this would be a small nongovernmental organization going against the policies of the government, with tremendous momentum already having been built up to induce other nations to follow the U.S. lead toward sanctions — and a possible war.

I first received assurances from the North Koreans that their invitation was still firm, that it was personally from their "Great Leader," and that I would be permitted to go directly from Seoul across the Demilitarized Zone (DMZ) to Pyongyang. Then I sent a letter to President Clinton stating that I had decided to make the trip. The president was still in Europe to commemorate the fiftieth anniversary of the Normandy landing, and my letter was directed to Vice President Al Gore. He convinced me to change its wording to "strongly inclined to go," with a promise to use his influence to get approval. I urged him to bypass the State Department, and the next day he called and said that Clinton had approved our trip, although he was certain the State Department would resent it.

Before going to Washington with Marion

and Rosalynn for a briefing, I wrote out a series of questions for use in North Korea, including information from on-site inspectors on the nuclear issue, possible easing of U.S.-DPRK relations, mutual inspection of military installations, presence of U.S. nuclear weapons in the area, U.S. obligations to South Korea, the status of joint military exercises between our two nations, and circumstances under which U.S. officials would deign to speak to their peers in Pyongyang. We had a brief meeting at the airport with National Security Adviser Anthony Lake, who was on his way to his home in New England and did not seem interested enough to spend much time with us or to see us at the White House. Our subsequent briefings from the CIA and State Department were superficial and in conflict with information that the Center's interns had gathered from Billy Graham, some university professors, CNN news reporters, and a few others who had visited North Korea in recent years. When I questioned the accuracy of statements from CIA and State Department people, they explained that no middle- or high-level U.S. official had ever visited North Korea and that they got their information from South Koreans and satellite observations.

We went home with many unanswered questions, including how we could communicate securely from Pyongyang to Washington without returning to South Korea; who would make the final decisions in North Korea — Kim Il Sung, his son Kim Jong Il, or military leaders; and who were the hawks and doves in Washington and what was their relative influence. I talked directly with those previously interviewed by our interns and an expert on nuclear engineering from Georgia Tech. At least I felt that I understood the basic agreements the United States desired to obtain from North Korea.

Before I left the next morning, I drafted a final list of questions to be answered in North Korea and ideas on how the crisis might be resolved. After I had read these to Bob Gallucci and obtained his approval, I decided to list a number of additional requests to be made of Kim Il Sung that might be "frosting on the cake."

We left home on Sunday, June 12, with no official status. We were on our own. We were welcomed to Seoul by U.S. Ambassador James Laney, a close friend and former president of Emory University. He had arranged talks with President Kim Young Sam and his top advisers, who seemed somewhat troubled about our planned visit to Pyongyang. One minister, who was in charge of reunification talks, seemed to be more objective about their northern neighbor and was quite helpful. Assuming a North Korean perspective, he gave us his assessment of the reasons for their troubling policies. General Gary Luck, commander of all U.S. and South Korean military forces, was deeply concerned about the consequences of a Korean war, which he thought was imminent. He estimated that the costs would far exceed those of the 1950s. He told us that he had given the same assessment to the president and top leaders in Washington earlier, but that his warnings were not received seriously, and military decisions were being made in Washington without consultation with him.

Colonel Forest Chilton told me that he could not work out an agreement for joint U.S. and North Korean teams to find and recover the remains of Americans killed in the Korean War. He believed his experts knew precisely where three thousand bodies were buried while our troops occupied the territory. I promised to discuss this with Kim Il Sung.

The crossing at Panmunjom was a strange and disturbing experience. For more than forty years, Koreans and Americans had stared across the Demilitarized Zone with suspicion, and often hatred and fear. We were the first persons permitted to cross the DMZ to and from Pyongyang since the armistice was signed in 1953! As we approached the precise line, a concrete pad about a foot wide, our aide Nancy Konigsmark stepped just across it to take our photograph. Instantly, she was grabbed by burly security guards and returned to the proper side.

North Korean vice foreign minister Song Ho Kyong was our host during the two-hour drive over an almost empty four-lane highway. He explained that his country did not produce luxury cars but made only buses, trains, subway cars, and trucks. We were to find a superb mass-transit system in Pyongyang, with an especially beautiful subway system (no graffiti) more than three hundred feet underground. Throughout our visit, our hosts were open, friendly, and remarkably careful not to make abusive or critical comments about the South Koreans. They often expressed concern about misunderstandings and lack of progress on the peninsula but would acknowledge that these had been caused by mutual mistakes.

We stayed in a beautiful guesthouse in a garden area adjacent to the Taedong River, and the North Korean officials readily agreed to our suggested schedule of discussions. Our first meeting was with Foreign Minister Kim Yong Nam, who was polite but whose responses to my proposal on how to end the impasse were quite hard-line. He had an apparent fixation on a round of talks with U.S. officials as a prerequisite to any affirmative actions. It seemed obvious that the threat of sanctions had no effect whatsoever, except as a pending insult, branding North Korea as an outlaw nation and their revered leader as a liar and criminal. This was something they could not accept.

Economic sanctions had no meaning for them, since their basic philosophy — almost a religion — is *ju-che,* meaning "self-reliance." In a practical sense, what was being proposed in the UN Security Council would not be damaging because North Korean trade with the United States and its allies was almost nonexistent and UN agencies provided the country with little benefit. Although the minister's comments were moderate in tone, it seemed quite likely that his country would go to war rather than yield to international condemnation and economic pressure, and he seemed uninterested in the specific proposals I had prepared.

I got up at three the following morning to try to decide what to do. Constrained by my

North Korean President Kim Il Sung greets President Carter and his wife, Rosalynn, during their visit to Pyongyang in 1994 for talks that helped to defuse a nuclear crisis on the peninsula. (THE CARTER CENTER)

agreements with Washington, I finally decided that Marion Creekmore should drive to Panmunjom to send a secure message from South Korea to inform Washington and seek authorization from President Clinton to propose a round of talks to defuse the crisis. In addition, I suggested that Bob Gallucci consider a visit to Korea. I woke Marion, he accompanied me into the garden to avoid any listening devices, and I gave him my message with instructions not to send it until I could meet later that morning with President Kim Il Sung.

When this meeting took place at the palace, Foreign Minister Kim and Vice Foreign Ministers Song Ho Kyong and Kang Sok Chu also attended. The latter was Gallucci's counterpart, responsible for negotiating with the United States on the nuclear issue.

President Kim was eighty-two years old but vigorous, alert, and remarkably familiar with the issues. He consulted frequently with his advisers, each of whom bounced up and stood erect while speaking to the "Great Leader." There was no doubt that Kim Il Sung was in full command and could make the final decisions. After thanking me for accepting his four-year-old invitation, he asked me to speak first.

I described my unofficial role, my briefings, and my visit with South Korean President Kim Young Sam, and then made the presentation that I had prepared before leaving home. I outlined the entire situation to be sure that he was fully aware of all concerns about North Korean nuclear policies. On occasion, he would nod or ask me to pause while he talked to his advisers. Richard Christenson, our State Department interpreter, later reported that Kim was obviously not thoroughly briefed on one important problem: International Atomic Energy Agency (IAEA) inspectors being expelled.

Finally, in effect, the president accepted all my proposals, with two major requests. One was that the United States support North Korea's acquisition of light water reactor technology, realizing that the funding and equipment could not come directly from America. (He had been promised a two-thousand-megawatt reactor by President Brezhnev in the late 1970s, but the Soviets had defaulted on this promise after Konstantin Chernenko became leader.) This was actually something we would have wanted the North Koreans to have because the enriched fuel would have to be acquired from foreign sources and the production of weapons-grade plutonium would not be so easy as in their old graphite-moderated reactor, which could use refined uranium from their own mines. Kim's second request was that the United States guarantee there would be no nuclear attack against his country. He wanted a third round of U.S.-DPRK talks to resolve all the outstanding nuclear issues. He was willing to freeze their nuclear program during the talks and to consider a permanent freeze if their aged reactors could be replaced with modern and safer ones. I was surprised to find Kim familiar with these detailed issues.

I assured him that there were no nuclear weapons in South Korea or tactical weapons in the waters surrounding the peninsula, and that I believed the United States would want to see the DPRK acquire light water reactors. He agreed with me that the entire Korean peninsula should be nuclear-free. Since I now felt that I had gotten everything we needed, Dick Christenson called Marion Creekmore to tell him to return to Pyongyang without sending any message to Washington.

After lunch, we moved to talks with Vice Minister Kang Sok Chu, the North Koreans' chief negotiator on nuclear questions. He went through the history of the nuclear issue from their point of view, which seemed reasonable in some respects. He was meticulous in his description of what had happened, and I could understand the correlation of events from totally disparate perspectives. On occasion, he deviated from what Kim Il Sung had committed to do, but when I asked him each time if he had a different policy from his "Great Leader," he would back down.

Kang claimed that they had delayed unloading the spent fuel rods from their Yongbyong reactor more than six months after the normal date and had been surprised by the IAEA's announcement to the UN Security Council, backed by the United States, that they had violated their agreement. He claimed they had made a reasonable proposal to resolve the issue, to which they never received a response.

Minister Kang informed me that when I arrived they had already decided to expel the inspectors and disconnect surveillance equipment in response to the abusive sanctions language announced by UN Ambassador Madeleine Albright and Bob Gallucci. Also, he said, "All the people in this country and our military are gearing up now to respond to those sanctions. If the sanctions pass, all the work you have done here will go down the drain." He said the North Koreans were convinced that the spent fuel rods could still be assessed by the IAEA and were willing to be flexible if this conviction should be proven wrong. He maintained that noted physicists in Europe and the United States agreed with their position. We discussed a number of other technical points. I saw no reason to argue with Kang on these points but just endeavored to protect the agreement I had reached with his president.

After supper, I called Bob Gallucci on an open line to report the apparent agreement with President Kim. He said they were having a high-level meeting in the White House and would "consider" my report. I notified him of my plan to give CNN an interview but to refrain from speaking for the U.S. government, and he had no objection. During the end of my live CNN interview, I was informed that National Security Adviser Tony Lake wanted to talk to me, and we finally got him on the phone. After I answered a few questions, he asked me to call him back in an hour for the U.S. decision. I did this, and he asked for three more hours to consult with other nations. This brought us to 5:30 A.M., and I understood that they would accept the terms I had worked out. Lake then read a statement they proposed to make, and he agreed to a few of my suggested changes. It was understood that the North Koreans would freeze their nuclear program through the new good-faith talks. In fact, it would be several months before the rods were cooled down enough for reprocessing and President Kim had agreed to "freeze" the nuclear program, as I suggested.

Later that morning (Friday in Korea, Thursday at home), Rosalynn, Marion Creekmore, Nancy Konigsmark, and I were invited to go on a long boat ride with President Kim and his wife, from Pyongyang down the Taedong River to the "barricade," a remarkable five-mile dam built by North Korean soldiers. An ingenious system of locks and dams permits shipping and the fresh river water to flow to the sea but impedes the influx of salt water. The CNN camera crew were also onboard. I advised Kim that, in my opinion, full implementation of our agreement would mean that the sanctions effort would be held in abeyance. (Unfortunately, part of this comment was picked up on camera and came out as though I were speaking for our government and declaring the sanctions issue to be dead.) I explained to the interpreter the meaning of *abeyance.*

We discussed removing the remains of U.S. soldiers buried during the war, and after I explained that this would avoid later arguments and be a significant goodwill gesture to the American people, the president listened to the comments of his wife and then agreed to permit joint teams to find and return these bodies, provided the United States paid the expenses. I urged him not to let this joint effort become bogged down in debates.

Things were going well, and I decided to push my luck. I asked him to agree to immediate summit talks with South Korean President Kim Young Sam to plan for reunification of the peninsula, to consider mutual reductions in military forces with joint inspections to confirm compliance, and to withdraw heavy armaments far enough from the DMZ to forgo a preemptive attack on Seoul. He agreed to all of these proposals.

Kim said that for forty years no progress had been made, and he asked if The Carter Center would be willing to provide our good services to bridge the existing gaps and to help ensure the success of North-South talks. I promised to mention all these things to President Kim Young Sam on my return to Seoul.

We found Kim Il Sung very open toward Christianity, having been saved from a Japanese prison in China by Christian pastors. Also he was an avid hunter (claiming to have killed two bears and two hundred boar during the past year) and quite interested in fishing. He and his wife argued about which of them was the better hunter. He said that after the Japanese were expelled from the country in 1945, the families along the rivers tried to kill all the "Japanese fish." He knew they were rainbow trout introduced before 1910 by American miners and had maintained a large program since then to stock the streams from several nurseries. We agreed that I would send in some biologists and fly-fishermen to analyze North Korea's fishing opportunities, and I let him know that Rosalynn and I would like to be among the first to fish the streams. After visiting the Children's Palace and seeing a remarkable performance of the young people's skill and talent, I finally went back to the guesthouse for some sleep.

The next morning we returned to the DMZ, where we had a press conference and answered questions from CNN, the North Korean news media, and reporters from China and Russia. Then we traveled with Ambassador Laney to Seoul, where I gave a full report to President Kim Young Sam. At the U.S. embassy, we were amazed to discover that our actions in North Korea had been met by criticism and partial rejection in Washington. I discussed this negative response on a secure telephone with Vice President Gore and told him I would like to come to Washington before going home to explain the results of my trip in more detail. I considered all my actions to have been in accord with the policies of the administration. Apparently coached from the sidelines, he made it clear that I should return directly to Plains and not brief the administration. After a discussion with Marion and Rosalynn, I decided to go to Washington anyway. It was obvious that either they did not understand what Kim and I had decided or their preference was some kind of further economic or military confrontation.

I held an extensive press conference at the U.S. embassy, during which Ambassador Laney informed me that President Kim Young Sam had agreed to the summit meeting. I explained the nuclear situation to the best of my ability, answered questions, and made it clear that I was still speaking as a private citizen representing The Carter Center.

When we landed in Portland, Oregon, to change planes, I had a call from Tom Johnson at CNN. He faxed us an incredibly negative article from *The Washington Post,* with quotes from top officials in the Clinton administration, such as, "We have no way of knowing why he thought what he thought, or why he said what he said." "Carter is hearing what he wants to hear, both from Kim Il Sung and from the administration. He is creating his own reality." The article also said that "when Carter first informed Washington of his desire to accept the North Korean invitation, officials were divided about whether to try to talk him out of it."

Marion Creekmore and I returned to Washington via Atlanta, while Rosalynn went home to Plains. No one met us at the airport or when we arrived at the White House, and we never saw the president, vice president, or any cabinet member. An usher took us to Tony Lake's office, where we found him, Bob Gallucci, Deputy National Security Adviser Sandy Berger, and Assistant Secretary of State Winston Lord. There was a strain in the air. I reminded them that I was well informed about the issues, not gullible, loyal to my president, and reasonably intelligent. I then read them the trip report I had written on the way home and answered their questions.

They explained that the remarks in *The Washington Post* (which they all denied making) were based on fragmentary information from Pyongyang. However, there was a more fundamental difference. The administration had been committed to what I considered a disastrous course of action — to browbeat North Korea publicly and to seek UN sanctions. I was doubtful that the Chinese would have permitted the resolution to pass and convinced that North Korea would not have yielded to this pressure, causing great danger of another Korean war.

Once the news report saying that, in my opinion, Kim Il Sung had responded adequately to U.S. proposals was broadcast, the sanctions movement was dead in the water. Influential people, both Republicans and Democrats, including Senator John McCain, were still calling for military action against North Korea. President Clinton, however, had made no criticism of me and had approved my trip over the objections of some of his top advisers, particularly in the State Department.

When I talked by secure phone to President Clinton, who was at Camp David, everyone left the room except Tony Lake. Clinton said he was grateful for my trip and appreciated the results, and I replied that he was the first person in the government who had said this. I briefed him for about thirty minutes, and when I hung up, Tony seemed distressed. He kept the door shut as we leveled with each other. He swore his friendship toward me, said he had approved my trip to Korea, and denied any responsibility for the criticisms. I repeated my differences with the administration and said I resented the White House decision that I should return from Seoul to Plains and not to Washington. When I made a brief report to the news media upon leaving the White House, Tony stood by my side to indicate support for what I had to say.

At my hotel I met with about a dozen reporters to give them basically the same report. Although most of the news stories were beginning to be more positive, I felt that I had to repair the potential damage of unanswered questions. After another extensive interview on CNN, I returned home. I had forgotten it was Father's Day.

South Korean Ambassador Han Seung Soo informed me that his country was assembling a top-level ministerial group to arrange for the summit meeting. Jim Laney called to say how grateful the South Koreans were for our defusing the crisis. Before my visit, people there had been flooding the stores to stock up on groceries and goods, and had held unprecedented air-raid drills and announced that 6 million reservists were being put on alert. After I came back to Seoul, everything had returned to normal.

There was still obvious skepticism in the White House and news media about my report of Kim Il Sung's commitments, so on Monday I sent Kim a letter, with a copy to Clinton, enumerating them all. He responded to me in writing on Wednesday, with a copy to the White House, confirming everything. I called Clinton, and he promised to announce that if the commitments were confirmed, there would be no need for sanctions.

A month later, Kim Il Sung died, and his son, Kim Jong Il, wrote to tell me that he would honor the commitments made by his father. Subsequently, Bob Gallucci was able to negotiate an official agreement with the North Koreans that confirmed the nuclear deal, and Secretary of State Madeleine Albright later visited Pyongyang. Kim Young Sam and his successor, Kim Dae Jung, were making good progress on reconciliation with North Korea.

And then a new administration came to Washington. President George W. Bush derided the North-South peace effort and, in effect, canceled the nuclear agreements with North Korea. He also ordained that there would be no face-to-face discussions with Pyongyang officials, and meetings with them would be confined to a six-nation forum.

Any commitment to forgo a military attack on the DPRK was out of the question until all other contentious issues were resolved. The North Koreans were accused of having a secret program to enrich uranium, a process that is very slow and requires an enormous facility of gaseous diffusion equipment or centrifuges. The North Koreans expelled the IAEA inspectors, renounced their commitment to the Non-Proliferation Treaty, and began processing spent fuel rods from the old Yongbyong nuclear reactor. They now have what is believed to be enough enriched nuclear material for seven or eight bombs, and have demonstrated their capability with one detected explosion.

HAITI

Our experiences in Haiti provided vivid proof that democracy is more than honest and fair elections.

We observed this neighbor of ours very closely in March 1990, when an army general, Hérard Abraham, overthrew the government and transferred executive power to the chief justice of the Supreme Court, Ertha Pascal-Trouillot. She called me after a few weeks to ask if The Carter Center would help ensure a free election by sending an observer mission.

Haiti had never known real democracy, having been ruled by "Papa Doc" Duvalier for twenty-six years and then by his son, "Baby Doc." Its citizens were terrorized by the Duvaliers' private army, the Tontons Macoutes, but a popular uprising finally forced Baby Doc to leave the country in 1986. An election was scheduled the following year. Early on Election Day, thirty-four citizens were assassinated by the Tontons Macoutes as they stood in line to vote. The army leaders (some of whom were alleged to have been involved in the attack) canceled the election.

This was the state of affairs when Rosalynn, Carter Center fellow Bob Pastor, and I went to Port-au-Prince to meet with President Pascal-Trouillot in July 1990. Security was still a concern, and we recommended that election observers from the United Nations and the Organization of American States be included. Calling on other members of the Center's Council of Freely Elected Heads of Government, we determined to assist Haiti with an election that was scheduled for the following December and formed a joint mission with the National Democratic Institute. It appeared that more responsible military officers were now in charge of security, and the Tontons Macoutes were relatively subdued. We paid a visit to the small courtyard where the thirty-four citizens had been murdered and found that a lively registration effort was under way, with future voting sites being set up as places for officials to sign up new voters. As an incentive, they were paid twenty-five cents for each name added to the rolls.

One of Baby Doc's ministers, Roger Lafontant, returned to Haiti in September and began to make incendiary speeches, encouraging the Tontons Macoutes to be more active. Lafontant had been accused of fomenting the violence that had aborted the previous election. The special focus of his anger was a young Catholic priest, Jean-Bertrand Aristide, who was a champion of Haiti's poorest and had never sought public office. A fiery orator and activist, Aristide angered many of Haiti's elites. He had been the target of several assassination attempts in the 1980s. In addition, his political activities and promotion of "liberation theology" were also unacceptable to Catholic Church officials, and he had been expelled from his Salesian religious order in 1988.

Aristide was an orphan who had been raised by Catholic nuns. They recognized a superb intelligence and made sure that he received a good education in Haiti, the Dominican Republic, Italy, and Israel. He had a special affinity for languages and was fluent in eleven. He also had a mystical reputation. Once he was riding in an automobile with four others when they were stopped by militants. He and his companions were forced out of the car, lined up, and mowed down with a submachine gun. Aristide was unscathed.

Eleven candidates were conducting a spirited campaign for president when Aristide, still a priest, decided at the last moment to seek the office. To the observers, it was clear that he was the overwhelming choice of the poor, who constituted a strong majority. Voter registration in some districts doubled almost overnight when he announced his candidacy. Aware of his past rhetoric, I went to see him, obtained his promise to abide by the laws and constitution of the country, and asked for his pledge to accept the results of the election. He was polite, but he refused to consider the possibility of another candidate's prevailing. He informed me that his supporters would not accept such a result.

Lafontant's supporters killed seven people and wounded fifty at an opposition political rally, but there were no serious problems on Election Day. A competent and honest general, Raoul Cédras, was in charge of security and worked closely with President Pascal-Trouillot and the international election observers. Rosalynn and I spent most of the day in Cité Soleil and other slum areas of Port-au-Prince, and we returned there for the vote count after the polls closed. It was an unforgettable experience. Large areas had no electricity, and the ballots had to be examined and tabulated by candlelight. Polling officials and observers from the various parties huddled around crude tables and called out ballot after ballot marked for Aristide. The nationwide tally gave him two-thirds of the total.

We returned to Haiti for the inauguration in February 1991 and found it difficult to reach the site, with hundreds of thousands of Haitians filling the streets and all public spaces in Port-au-Prince. All of us shared the excitement as Aristide made an eloquent speech promising opportunities for the poor, a peaceful society, and a new era of accommodation between his followers and former enemies, even the Tontons Macoutes.

Tragically, the priest had little practical judgment about how to govern, and the nation was soon divided as deeply as ever. Aristide found it impossible to compromise on any issue and was unwilling to consult with business, professional, educational, or social leaders. Instead of forming a working relationship with military leaders, the new president formed his own loyal security force. He was at odds on most major issues with recently elected members of the parliament, so urgently needed reform legislation was stalemated. We offered several times to help arrange consultations to alleviate the problems, but Aristide never responded to us.

After only eight months of this administration, a coup was planned. General Cédras came to the president's office, protected him from assassination, and escorted him to the airport, where a plane was waiting to take him to exile in Venezuela. He soon moved to the United States, where he spent three years seeking international support. During this time, both Aristide and Cédras urged The Carter Center to mediate the dispute between them, but I could not obtain approval from Washington to do so.

There was bloodshed in Haiti during this time. Finally, the United Nations and the Organization of American States negotiated what was known as the Governors Island Accord between Aristide and Cédras; it called for sustained dialogue, nomination of a prime minister by the president to be confirmed by a reconstituted parliament, suspension of sanctions against Haiti, an amnesty for the military and police, establishment of a new police force, and the return of Aristide to Haiti in October 1993. Each side blamed the other when the accord was not implemented.

The UN Security Council finally resolved in July 1994 to deploy a multinational force to Haiti, and President Clinton said U.S. forces would lead it. President Aristide, now four years into his elected six-year term, would thus be returned to office through the use of force. I was informed that thirty thousand American troops had been marshaled to invade Haiti and that General Cédras wished to talk with me. We spoke on September 14. With his approval, we made a transcript of our telephone conversations; below are selected quotations from his statement in French, as translated by his brother Alex, along with my responses:

Cédras: The U.S. sanctions are causing genocide among the world's poorest people here in Haiti. President Clinton's solution is the worst of all possible ones. It is very important that you come to Haiti, to see what is going on and help work out a solution.

JC: I have been in Haiti seven times and

am deeply concerned about the people. I do not represent the U.S. government, but it is necessary for me to tell you the truth. An irrevocable decision has been made to invade Haiti unless you and the two other leaders are prepared to leave. It will be helpful if you also welcome the UN forces to come in to preserve order.

Cédras: The Governors Island Accord has been violated in many ways by both sides. Now we have a purely civilian government under President Emile Jonassaint, the most respected public servant in Haiti. If the invasion decision is irrevocable, I must obey my civilian government and defend my people in accordance with the Haitian constitution.

Our conversation was interrupted by a call from the White House. I told President Clinton that I had been talking to Cédras and described our conversation. Clinton approved further conversations and suggested that I concentrate on Cédras's departure and make him know that the United States was determined to put Aristide back in power.

Cédras called me again.

Cédras: Aristide has no vision of democracy. He burned nineteen of our soldiers to death in January 1991 and then claimed it was God's will. Since Governors Island, I have been trying to modernize the Haitian army based on the agreement, but I have received only $35,000 for this purpose. Our children are dying from the American embargo. U.S. universities are reporting that only one thousand of our children die each month from starvation, but this figure is more than a year old. The situation is much worse now.

JC: The bottom line is that you must leave Haiti, and you can come to our country or another of your choice. Then I or an acceptable delegation could meet with the group of leaders to plan a peaceful implementation of the Governors Island agreement, including Aristide's return. UN forces could come in as agreed, in a harmonious way, to help preserve peace. I will meet with you after you leave Haiti, if you desire.

Cédras: My leaving is not the important issue. No one in Haiti has a guarantee of safety if Aristide returns. People in all 560 sections of the nation face his supporters, poised for violence.

JC: Let me close by saying that I will report to President Clinton that you are not willing to leave because you are convinced that massive civil violence will result. You should know that the result of this decision is that an invasion will occur. You can call me at any time if the circumstances change.

I talked to Senator Sam Nunn of Georgia, chairman of the Armed Services Committee, who was strongly opposed to an invasion and planned to demand that the president get full approval from the Congress before launching what inevitably would be a long and costly occupation of Haiti. Sam said he would be willing to go to Haiti with me and would call back later with a suggested Republican, perhaps Senator Richard Lugar of Indiana. I suggested instead retired general Colin Powell, and asked Sam to have him call me. When General Powell called, he said the best approach would be full cooperation between the military leaders of the United States and Haiti.

President Clinton called again to tell me that he was interested in my further conversations with Cédras. He thought they had some nibbles from Cedras's aide, Brigadier

General Philippe Biamby and General Joseph Michel François, head of the Port-au-Prince police, the two other leaders under pressure to leave, but he wasn't sure. He said they would have to stick to the invasion timetable unless Cédras would leave. He wanted Cédras to know that congressional demands or adverse opinion polls in the United States would not affect this decision. He understood Cédras's concerns about the need to maintain order in Haiti. On the line was $1.2 billion in aid, which was dependent on Aristide's return and Cédras's departure. Clinton was prepared to let the chairman of the Joint Chiefs of Staff, General John Shalikashvili, and National Security Adviser Tony Lake call Cédras if I thought the time was right.

I outlined my conversations with Nunn, Powell, and others, and told the president we were willing to go to Haiti if Cédras would agree to leave. Somewhat tentatively, the president said that this would be possible, but only if Cédras agreed in advance to leave.

I gave Alex Cédras this message to deliver to his brother: "If you will agree to leave in accordance with the Governors Island Accord, I will put together a delegation of distinguished Americans, including U.S. senators and General Colin Powell, and come to Haiti to meet with you, President Jonassaint, and other Haitian leaders to resolve the present crisis and to plan for the future of Haiti. If we are unsuccessful after a few days, we will make an accurate and balanced report of the results."

Senator Nunn called a couple of hours later to report that the president had asked if he was willing to go to Haiti with me, and if he intended to call General Powell. Tony Lake phoned at about 6:00 P.M. to say that Clinton would contact me after his televised speech that evening, which would address the Haiti crisis. Cédras did not phone me, but he responded to the president's very critical speech by pledging on CBS to die in defense of his country.

President Clinton called at 11:15 P.M. to ask me to talk to Cédras in the morning to "see if he would receive your delegation." I asked him several times if this meant that he wanted us to go even without a firm prior commitment for Cédras to leave, and Clinton responded in general terms that this was what he wanted but that I should get the best response from Cédras and report the results to him before he would make a final decision. He said, "We must go the second mile," and "We need to do it like we did in Korea."

The next day, Colin Powell and Sam Nunn agreed to go with me to Haiti, but Colin asked that we wait until Saturday morning if possible. They informed me that the president wanted General Shalikashvili and Secretary of State Warren Christopher to go, but Sam, Colin, and I thought this would be a mistake. It would remove our flexibility because no official in the administration would be able even to speak to the "illegal" government leaders, who included both Cédras and Jonassaint. I expressed our concern to Tony Lake.

When Cédras called, I read him this statement:

You are aware of the clear goals of the United Nations and the U.S. government. President Clinton has authorized a visit to Haiti by me, Senator Sam Nunn, and former Chief of Staff General Colin Powell to work with you, other members of the military, business and governmental leaders, including Mr. Jonassaint, to devise a peaceful and mutually acceptable way to achieve these clear goals. I need your pledge immediately to cooperate and arrange the necessary meetings, so that we can plan to make the trip tomorrow.

He replied that he would have to consult with President Jonassaint, who would make the final decision, but that the government had already indicated a desire for meetings. Later, President Clinton called me and said he had always supported the very things we had suggested: a limited delegation, flexible talking points, and our ability to talk to anyone in Haiti. He said that the Department of Defense was also fully supportive but didn't mention State. Sam and Colin reported that some of the top State Department officials "went up in smoke" about our delegation.

Before we departed on a military plane on Saturday morning, September 17, a press statement was issued from Washington saying that a delegation of American leaders would visit Port-au-Prince and that their mission would be to make a final effort during a brief period to find a peaceful way to implement the basic terms of the Governors Island Accord, which had been negotiated and signed by Haitian President Jean-Bertrand Aristide and General Raoul Cédras.

In Port-au-Prince, we went to the military command headquarters, where we found all the Haitian generals and their four senior colonels assembled. Bob Pastor was with us, with a portable computer on which he would be keeping a record of the proceedings. It almost took force to exclude two junior State Department representatives and Ambassador William Swing from the room. I first outlined our mission in detail and answered a few questions from General Cédras and the others. Cédras repeated all the arguments he had made to me during our extended telephone conversations.

Then, as previously agreed, I asked General Powell to describe the differences between the military capabilities of Haiti and the United States. He outlined potential invasion plans so formidable that we all sat with our mouths open. There were to be massive waves of Navy SEALs, landing craft, paratroopers, armored vehicles and artillery, and aircraft of all kinds. Later, Sam said that Colin had described weapons that neither he nor any member of the Senate Armed Services Committee had ever heard mentioned before.

After a long silence, Cédras changed the subject. He said that lower-level officers had orchestrated and carried out the coup in September 1991 and that the soldiers were prepared to kill Aristide. He said, "I put my body before his, so that they would have to kill me first. After we got him out of the country, they offered me the presidency, but

I refused, saying that the parliament is in charge." He added, "The U.S. government is not in favor of this effort today. Ambassador Swing notified us this morning that you would meet with us only ten minutes, to deliver an ultimatum, with our position then to be heard only through the media statements. In his speech Thursday night, President Clinton made some accusations against me that were truly incredible, perhaps even to the American public. There is a lot of violence here. We cannot control every street in Haiti with our people in great tension, ancient animosities coming to the surface, with only 7,000 men, no spare parts or fuel for our vehicles, and 560 sections in the country to be pacified."

While Sam, Colin, and Bob continued meeting with this group, I went to my room in the hotel and wrote a draft agreement, which the four of us went over carefully to be sure that it was compatible with our instructions from the White House and that it encompassed some of the legitimate concerns of the generals with whom we had met.

We all reconvened after supper, and from 10:30 P.M. to about 2:15 A.M. we and the generals discussed our written proposal. They had a number of questions, and we made a few minor changes to my text. When we adjourned for the night, I stopped for a private meeting with Cédras, telling him that I would like to meet his family. He replied, "So would I, since I haven't seen them for several days. Yesterday was my son's tenth birthday and I wasn't there. I'm going home now, to see them and get some rest."

I woke up early Sunday morning and called Rosalynn on the satellite phone to tell her that we were not making much progress. She said that I should take the initiative and go see Mrs. Cédras, who she had heard was quite influential. Rosalynn also understood that the Cédrases were deeply religious — both Methodists, she thought. I woke up Bob Pastor, who also had had about two hours' sleep, and told him to call Alex Cédras to see if the general would let me visit his home. Before Bob could make my request, Alex said, "The general wants the Carter delegation to come by his home to meet his family."

We had a breakfast meeting scheduled with key Aristide supporters at the ambassador's residence, but when we arrived they were not there. Since we had met with members of the "coup government," Ambassador Swing told us that Aristide's people refused to see us. Then, at about 8:15, we went to the Cédras home, where the general welcomed us with his wife, Yannick, his seventeen-year-old son, thirteen-year-old daughter, and ten-year-old son. I congratulated his younger son and gave him a little Carter Center pocketknife as a birthday present. While he sat beside me on the couch, their daughter brought in a photograph of her and me, taken and inscribed during the 1990 election. Then Yannick dismissed the children. She was well dressed, perfectly groomed, and intense.

She made a long speech and didn't accept any interruptions. When we did respond with a few words, she paid no attention. She talked about the grandeur of Haiti, the courage and pride of its people, the service of her ancestors, the suffering of her nation because of poverty and strife, and the inability of Haitian patriots to accept defeat. She reported that she and her children had taken an oath the night before to die rather than leave their home. She had seen American Delta squads scouting their house on several occasions and knew it was targeted. (This was confirmed by a major in our Special Forces.) She thought the house was to be destroyed, but the surveillance was probably so that Cédras could be apprehended if the invasion forced him into hiding.

We thought that our mission was surely over, but I looked at Colin, and he described the obligation of a commander when faced with insuperable odds: to consider the well-being of those under him and not just his own preferences and glory. This statement made a profound impression. Then I spoke about the ease of waging war versus the difficulty of waging peace and briefly restated the arguments I had made. Mrs. Cédras and her husband looked at each other. There was a long silence, and then the general said, "We will meet you later in our headquarters. We have some responses to your written proposal."

We went to the presidential palace and met the eighty-one-year-old Emile Jonassaint, whom I had known from 1990, when he was chairman of the Council of State. He asked to see me alone, and Colin, Sam, and Bob went into the next room to meet with the provisional cabinet members. Jonassaint was tall, very black, gangly, and quite at ease. He expressed support for our mission and said that Haiti would choose peace, not war. He asked me to come back to see him if there were any problems. It was obvious that he was not a puppet leader propped up by the army generals.

We met again with the officers in their command headquarters, and they presented us with an alternate draft, in English. Our original proposal was relatively intact, but slowly we agreed on a few basic changes, involving the coordination between U.S. and Haitian armed forces and the insertion of the officers' requirement to leave when a general amnesty was approved by the parliament. This was compatible with the Governors Island Accord.

We faxed a copy of the new draft to President Clinton, and at about 2:00 P.M. he and I discussed the text. There were two key problems: the timing of the officers' departure from office and the question of who could sign the agreement on behalf of Haiti. The latter was especially troubling. The United States was demanding that Cédras, not Jonassaint, sign. The president said we would have only one more hour — maximum — before leaving Haiti.

The Haitian foreign minister, Charles David, came over and assumed surprising authority in making changes in the document, even without approval from the generals. We went back to the headquarters room and sat waiting for a response from Washington. Suddenly, Brigadier General Biamby charged into the room carrying a portable telephone. We all turned to him and he said, "We have just been informed from Fort Bragg, North Carolina, that soldiers

Former U.S. senator Sam Nunn (D-Ga.) and former chairman of the Joint Chiefs of Staff Colin Powell joined President Carter in a negotiation that led to the departure of Haiti's de facto leaders and averted a U.S.-led multinational invasion. (THE ASSOCIATED PRESS)

have been instructed to don their parachutes and head this way. You all have betrayed us. We cannot trust you. This has been just a front, to keep all of us commanders in this room with our troops at ease while your forces attack our country. I am taking my commanding officer to a secure command headquarters, and we will alert our forces."

I was desperate and angry. I made an emotional speech to Cédras and the others, saying that we knew nothing of the U.S. attack and that the generals had also betrayed me. I had trusted them to have the best interests of their people at heart and had reported their unselfishness. Now I realized that all they wanted was to stay in office a few more weeks. They were willing to sacrifice their own men and the peaceful existence of the people they were supposed to defend. I said that I was disgusted with them. I also said that no one in America had ever asked me to come to Haiti; I had come because I was concerned about the same people the generals were supposed to be protecting. Yesterday I had been ashamed to learn that the U.S.-UN embargo had caused permanent mental and physical damage to thousands of Haitian children. Now the generals and I were in the same boat, ensuring the further suffering of the same people by giving up on the only peace option available.

They were taken aback. They huddled to consider the situation and then suggested that we visit President Jonassaint, who would decide if they had to leave as I had proposed. Colin told me, for the first time, that the military operation was, indeed, already under way. We were in the Haitian military headquarters, protected by troops on the balcony and throughout the building, and confronting a mob of several thousand people who were growing increasingly restless and antagonistic. It was about 4:30 P.M., I think, when we undertook what we thought was a desperate and fruitless mission. Moving rapidly, the generals and our delegation all slipped out the back door of the building, got in armored vehicles, and rode around the huge crowd in the square and over to the presidential palace. We forgot Bob Pastor, who had to pack the computer and printer, and he was left behind. He ran across the square to the palace.

President Jonassaint welcomed us. I sat beside him on the couch, with General Cédras, Major General Jean-Claude Duperval, and a colonel across from us. The ministers of defense, foreign affairs, and information were on our right, and Sam, Colin, and Bob were on our left. The interpreter bent over behind Jonassaint and me. When I explained the situation to the president, he replied, "As I told you earlier, Haiti will accept peace, not war."

Instantly, the ministers jumped up and said, "We will not accept this decision." The defense minister said, "I respect you as my father but will not serve under you anymore. You will have my resignation tomorrow morning." Jonassaint, completely relaxed, replied, "And I'll accept it. We already have a weak government, and your departure won't weaken it much further." The information minister, who was the most fervent of all, said, "I'll assemble the entire cabinet in the next room, to determine what our decision will be." Jonassaint replied, "The decision has already been made."

I went to tell President Clinton that we had an agreement, and he replied, "Thank God! Thank God!"

There were two more tasks to perform: Cédras's personal acknowledgment of Jonassaint's authority and the signing of official documents. When I asked Cédras, he took it as an insult, but Colin stood and said firmly that we had to make a report to the military officers of the multinational force and must have a firm answer from the commanding general of Haiti's forces. Cédras stood at attention, his hat under his left arm, and said, "On my honor as a soldier, I will abide by my president." General Duperval made the same statement.

However, we had another problem. Jonassaint would not agree that Cédras should sign the agreement on behalf of Haiti. "Contrary to what has been written in America to slander our country, this is not a military dictatorship," he said. I went back to the phone and asked the president to permit me to sign with Jonassaint, making the argument that he was the president of those with whom we had been negotiating and had in fact made the final decision. Clinton finally agreed, provided I make it plain that this did not imply diplomatic recognition of Jonassaint's provisional government.

When I returned to the president's office, I stretched the facts somewhat by saying, "President Clinton will be pleased to have you sign the document. I will sign for him on behalf of the United States, and you for the provisional government. However, you must realize that this does not imply diplomatic recognition." He smiled and said that he understood this perfectly. I signed the agreement and passed it over to him. He glanced at it and said, "I cannot sign just an English-language version of our agreement.

There must be copies in both languages."
I turned to our interpreter and urged him
to translate the document as rapidly as possible. We knew that our paratroopers were
approaching Haiti. I asked the interpreter
Larry Rossin to check the accuracy of the
translation.

I went back down the long hall and took
the phone from General Jerry Bates, to report to Clinton that all questions had been
resolved and that we would be signing the
agreement in a few minutes. He said for us
to leave immediately.* The delay seemed
endless, but we finally received French and
English versions, and Jonassaint and I both
signed the documents.

After consulting with President Jonassaint,
the foreign minister said they had one specific request: that I ask American officials
to stop the vituperative attacks on those
with whom we had reached the agreement.
I agreed to do so, went down the long hall
again, and repeated the request to President
Clinton. He replied, "Yes, I will do this, but
I can't control everyone in Washington." I

*We learned later that, at this point, he ordered
sixty-one C-130s to turn around in midair and go
back to Pope Air Force Base in North Carolina.
They had been flying for seventy-five minutes.

wanted Bob Pastor to remain in Haiti to report to me on the arrival of U.S. troops, so I requested that he be permitted to stay at the U.S. embassy residence and have some transportation. Clinton agreed, and I assured Bob that this would be done. The secretary of state sent word through the Secret Service that I was not to make any statement to the news media. I won't reveal my immediate response, which I then asked not to be delivered with the expletives.

The Secret Service agents told me that they had packed my clothes and files at the hotel and my suitcase was at the airport. (Later, at the White House, I found in my bag the hotel's soap, washcloths, bug spray, air freshener, and everything else that was not nailed down.) We then hurried to the airport, bade everyone good-bye, and left for Washington. Colin ordered rum and Coke for our delegation, and we toasted one another and compared notes on what had been among the most interesting thirty hours of our lives.

Although we received assurances that all departments in the administration and also President Aristide were fully supportive of the agreement we had worked out, Mrs. Cédras called three weeks later to report on behalf of her husband that there was little cooperation between the U.S. forces and the Haitian leaders and that no progress had been made concerning the amnesty or honorable retirement for General Cédras and others. They also needed assistance in leasing their private property.

After Nicaragua had refused to receive the Haitian military leaders, President Ernesto Pérez Balladares of Panama invited them, provided Aristide would write a letter approving their presence in his country. I talked to Aristide, who agreed with my request, thanked me profusely for going to Haiti, and said he had made a public statement in support of the Panama offer.

I called the State Department, and Deputy Secretary of State Strobe Talbott insisted that the Cédras family go to El Salvador, saying that the Panamanians could not be trusted. He also acknowledged that they had not asked Aristide to write a letter to President Balladares.

I objected strongly and finally reached an agreement with everyone so that the Cédrases' property could be leased and they could proceed to Panama about four weeks after our visit to Port-au-Prince. Aristide finished out his term in office and was reelected in 2000, in an election boycotted by the opposition. However, in February 2004 he was ousted again by armed gangs and popular protests and taken from the country. He claimed that he was kidnapped by the U.S. government and removed to South Africa. (The United States neither confirmed nor denied these allegations but has insisted that Aristide left willingly.) Later he returned to Jamaica, but American officials considered this too close to Haiti, so Aristide now resides in South Africa.

Sudan and Uganda

There are few countries in which The Carter Center has concentrated more effort than Sudan. This enormous country, equal in size to all the states east of the Mississippi River, has been torn apart by an internecine war for more than twenty years. In addition, the southern three provinces, controlled by a revolutionary group known as the Sudan People's Liberation Army/Movement (SPLA/M), was a hotbed of Guinea worm and river blindness, diseases that we targeted to be controlled or eradicated.

Unfortunately, there was a stalemate in progress toward peace and the accomplishment of our health goals. The governments of Sudan in Khartoum and Uganda in Kampala were at odds and had severed diplomatic relations for five years. Each ac-

Sudan President Omar al-Bashir and Uganda President Yoweri Museveni shake hands after sealing the Nairobi Agreement negotiated in 1999 by President Carter and the Center's Conflict Resolution Program. The countries committed to stop supporting forces against each other's government and agreed to eventually reestablish full diplomatic relations between them, opening the door for improved regional peacemaking.
(THE CARTER CENTER)

cused the other of supporting revolutionary groups.

Sudan claimed that President Yoweri Museveni was permitting his Ugandan forces to strengthen the SPLA/M forces of John Garang in their revolutionary war that had begun (in its most recent form) in 1983. Having traveled extensively in the region and having met Garang a few times in Uganda, I was fairly certain that the allegation was justified. For his part, Museveni accused the Sudanese of giving assistance to the Lord's Resistance Army (LRA), a paramilitary group that was based in Southern Sudan and invaded northern Uganda regularly to attack villages, rape and kill adults, and kidnap children. The boys were forced to be trained in committing military atrocities, and the girls became either concubines or wives of the LRA troops. The LRA leader was Joseph Kony, who proclaimed himself to be a spirit medium dedicated to imposing his version of the Ten Commandments on the portions of Uganda that he coveted. President Omar al-Bashir always denied vehemently that he condoned or assisted these strange forces, but he resisted Ugandan troops crossing his nation's borders in pursuit of Kony's forces.

The two leaders refused to talk to each

other to resolve these complex differences, and for several years I explored with them the possibility of having The Carter Center negotiate a peace agreement. Finally, having received tacit approval from John Garang, I was also able to persuade the presidents to meet, with The Carter Center serving as mediator.

In December 1999, our director of peace programs, Ambassador Gordon Streeb, and I traveled to Nairobi, where our negotiating team of Dr. Joyce Neu, Tom Crick, and Vincent Farley had been having preliminary meetings with subordinate officials from Uganda and Sudan at the Windsor Golf and Country Club near the city. President Bashir arrived shortly thereafter, and I met with him and Sudanese Ambassador Mahdi Ibrahim, whom I had known for many years. I listened to their complaints and proposals and demanded that they continue to restrain Joseph Kony and his Lord's Resistance Army, return all abducted children possible, and cooperate with peace efforts of the group of nations in East Africa known as the Inter-Governmental Authority on Development (IGAD). Then I went through the same procedure with the Ugandan officials, which gave me a good understanding of the differences between the two nations and some ideas for possible compromises.

Following my usual procedure, I then went to my room, consulted with our Carter Center team, and typed the most substantive and balanced text I could devise. This would be a "single document" that I would reluctantly modify as required to accommodate the determined insistence of the two presidents. Knowing there was only this draft, neither side could suspect that I was misleading them, and I would modify the text on my portable computer and print out two identical copies. I knew that each concession would be made only if there was a conviction that benefits would outweigh costs, and that the final agreement would have to be seen as beneficial to both sides.

The next morning, when President Museveni arrived from Uganda, I went over my proposals with him and then went back and forth between the two presidents for the rest of the day. The final agreement included these main points, which, in retrospect, seemed self-evident:

"Each nation will respect the sovereignty and territorial integrity of the other, renounce the use of force to resolve differences, and will take steps to prevent any hostile actions against each other;

"Both will make every effort to disband and disarm terrorist groups and prevent any acts of terrorism or hostile actions that might endanger the security of the other nation;

"Neither side will harbor, sponsor, or give military or logistical support to any rebel groups, or hostile elements from each other's territories;

"Both will join in a common effort to promote regional peace, both on their own initiative and in full support of IGAD's role in bringing an end to the civil war in Sudan;

"Both will refrain from hostile and negative propaganda campaigns against each other;

"All prisoners of war will be returned to their respective nations;

"Both condemn any abuse or injury of innocent citizens, and will make a special effort to locate any abductees, especially children, and return them to their families. All information about such cases will be shared with The Carter Center, UNICEF, and other international organizations, and both sides will cooperate fully in the search and rescue of these victims;

"Both will honor international laws governing refugees, NGO activities, and cross-border transportation, and facilitate the return or resettlement of refugees in accordance with UN High Commissioner for Refugees regulations;

"Amnesty and reintegration assistance will be offered to all former combatants who renounce the use of force;

"If all other terms of this agreement are honored satisfactorily, offices will be opened within a month of this date in both capital cities, and junior diplomatic personnel will be assigned for service. By the end of February 2000, ambassadors will be exchanged and full diplomatic relations restored."

We decided to go to Nairobi to have a formal signing ceremony at Kenyan President Daniel arap Moi's office, with him and me witnessing the agreement.

The next morning I met at length with the two presidents to reconfirm what we had decided and to prepare for implementation of the agreement.

It was obvious to everyone that the main purpose of U.S. State Department policy was to harass the Arab regime in Khartoum and to refrain from offering any help for the effort to bring peace to Sudan. Despite this, the African leaders now saw improved hope for progress in the Sudan peace effort, which would have to encompass freedom of worship and self-determination for the people in Southern Sudan, an end to the long and bloody war, the return of displaced families to their homes, a fair sharing of the nation's wealth, and assistance in rebuilding their lives. We believed these goals were within reach if the East African peace process could gain adequate support from the international community. We hoped that the near future would bring peace to the suffering people of Sudan — almost 2 million of whom had perished in the most vicious of all existing wars.

Before leaving Nairobi, I enjoyed visiting with my friends Richard and Meave Leakey. Along with other members of their family, they had been preeminent among the paleontologists who had made the most significant fossil discoveries in Ethiopia, Kenya, and Tanzania. Later, our tired and overworked staff went with me to the remarkable Kenya National Museum, where Meave gave us a lecture and used the Leakey family's original hominid artifacts to illustrate how human life has developed during the past 5 million years.

After returning home, I sent my usual trip report and then had a call from Secretary of State Madeleine Albright. After repeating what had happened in Nairobi, I said that I believed the ill-advised U.S. policy was at least partially responsible for the continuing war in Sudan. She asked if I would help them revise what she herself characterized as a "flawed policy" of attempting to eliminate the Arab regime in Khartoum, blaming all the nation's problems on the leaders there, and preventing substantive peace talks to end the north-south conflict. Despite our best efforts, these goals prevailed throughout the administration's time in office. We could only look to the future.

There were many hard feelings following the disputed 2000 U.S. presidential election. I felt very strongly that Al Gore had both won the nationwide vote and prevailed in Florida, but our intense hope for a substantive peace effort in Sudan overcame my partisan prejudices. Rosalynn and I decided to attend the inauguration ceremonies in Washington after five Republican Supreme Court justices declared George W. Bush to be the winner. Some people commented that we were the only voluntary Democrats present on the reviewing platform, and the

SEEKING NEW PATHS TO PEACE IN SUDAN

Mary Biba Philip, former mayor of Yei, Rumbek, in Southern Sudan, says, "We want peace that is born from the grass roots." (ALEX LITTLE)

Every day, villagers would find Mary Biba Philip sitting under a tree in the center of town. There, they shared their host of problems with her, seeking her intervention and advice. As mayor of the town of Yei, in war-torn Southern Sudan, Philip had her hands full, but she made certain to see everyone who wanted to talk to her. Day in, day out, Philip was reminded of the effects on her people of the civil war that raged for almost two decades.

"We want peace, peace that is born from grass roots so everybody will know it is their peace," she said. "Then they will sustain the peace; they will own it so there will not be conflict or violence again."

Mary Biba Philip had a distinguished status in Southern Sudan as the only female local government official at the rank of mayor or higher. She never hesitated to criticize the use of child soldiers to the army generals. Her outspokenness and prominence in the community led her colleagues to tap her to participate in a workshop on conflict resolution skills presented by The Carter Center.

Mayor Philip joined other local government officials, top leaders from the rebel Sudan People's Liberation Army/Movement, and representatives from nongovernmental organizations in learning relevant skills, such as how to build a constituency, the role of mediators and how to communicate with them, and alternative dispute resolution methods. The lack of a civil society structure often leads to ad hoc governance methods and to conflict itself. In such an environment, training helps prepare better leaders and community activists.

"We learned how to negotiate to solve our conflicts," Philip said. "Now we have the knowledge."

That workshop and one presented by The Carter Center for a similar group in Khartoum prepared the warring parties to participate in peace talks convened in 2002 by the Inter-Governmental Authority on Development, an East African body mandated to lead peace efforts in the country. Nearly three years later, in January 2005, the government of Sudan and the Sudan People's Liberation Army/ Movement signed a historic peace agreement, bringing an end to Africa's longest-running civil war.

This skill-building workshop augmented low-key but ongoing work by the Center for more than a decade to help resolve the Sudanese conflict and improve the climate for a just and lasting peace in this country. Since independence in 1956, more than 2 million people have died and more than twice that number have been forced from their homes during civil war. Many of these deaths were from famine and disease, exacerbated by the social upheaval of conflict.

The "Guinea worm cease-fire" that we negotiated in 1995 was a classic example of the interrelationship of the twin human rights of peace and health around which The Carter Center organizes its program agenda. A then-unprecedented period of nearly six months of relative peace allowed health workers to enter areas of Sudan previously inaccessible due to fighting. Interventions brought the first treatments to prevent Guinea worm in Southern Sudan, pills to prevent river blindness, and expanded child immunizations. For many years after that, we still struggled to overcome Guinea worm in Sudan, which had the most cases of any country. But the second peace agreement, in 2005, has allowed rapid intervention and the promise that this disease will soon be eradicated not only for the Sudanese but for the global community.

Bush family expressed their appreciation for our attendance. I approached President Bush immediately after the ceremony and told him I had one request: that he make an effort to bring peace to Sudan.

He promised to do so and suggested that I meet with his secretary of state, Colin Powell, and national security adviser, Condoleezza Rice, after giving them a few weeks to become settled in their offices. Two months later, John Hardman and I went to the State Department and renewed our request, offering the services of The Carter Center or our assistance to any other group whom President Bush might designate to bring peace to Southern Sudan.

The president kept his promise and chose former senator John Danforth of Missouri as his special emissary. With great assistance from a distinguished general from Kenya, Lazaro Sumbeiywo, an international effort was successful in bringing an end to Sudan's twenty-one-year civil war. Although it is a fragile peace, it has ended the intense strife there and made it possible for our health programs to proceed throughout the southern region.

BOSNIA AND HERZEGOVINA

Our first involvement with Bosnia-Herzegovina was in June 1994, when Chris

Spiro, former speaker of the New Hampshire House of Representatives, brought Serbian Ambassador Milan Milutinović to our home in Plains to deliver a personal message from President Slobodan Milošević. In summary, it said that he was ready to conclude a comprehensive settlement in the Balkans but needed to be treated with respect by the U.S. government. I knew that the European-UN peace effort had reached a dead end, and there was no confidence that the Europeans would enforce an agreement even if one were reached.

The lack of progress was due to the fact that the United States had not played a strong role, imposing rather than just proposing a comprehensive peace. The main message was that Milošević wanted me to come to Belgrade, representing either The Carter Center or the U.S. government. I responded that there were multiple channels for peace and that I had no desire to become involved in the Balkans. I relayed his message to President Clinton.

The situation continued to deteriorate, and our Center began to monitor developments very carefully, primarily using the services of our interns. We subsequently became involved, to help prevent an all-out war and multiple human rights violations. Our work in this area was an intriguing experience that involved three men who have since been indicted for war crimes and genocide by the International Criminal Tribunal in The Hague. One of them (Milošević) was arrested and died during his trial. The other two are now international fugitives, with $5 million bounties, offered by the U.S. government, on their heads.

Early in December 1994, I received a handwritten letter from the Bosnian Serb political leader, Radovan Karadžić, requesting I meet with a delegation to explore ways for the Serbs to accept the latest recommendations of the International Contact Group (United States, United Kingdom, France, Germany, Italy, and Russia). I was not very familiar with the political situation in the former area of Yugoslavia, although I had welcomed Marshal Tito to the White House for a formal visit.

Rosalynn and I still remember the thirty-five-minute toast that he gave after the state banquet, which then had to be translated into English. At that time, multiple ethnic and political groups constituted Yugoslavia, and Tito was holding them together with his political shrewdness, the power of his personality, and his reputation as a hero who had resisted the Nazis during World War II and later defied Stalin and the Soviets.

After Tito's death, in May 1980, Rosalynn and I were the first visitors to Yugoslavia to meet with the ruling committee, which we found fragmented and confused. Ethnic tensions grew as the peoples of the republics of Slovenia, Croatia, Kosovo, and Serbia made conflicting demands for power and autonomy.

Radovan Karadžić was a poet and a psychiatrist who was accused of holding some UN hostages and was growing increasingly independent from Slobodan Milošević, the elected ruler of the Serbs, who also sought dominion over the other provinces. In April 1992, Bosnia had come to be recognized as an independent state, and Karadžić became the first president of the Bosnian Serb administration, with its capital in the mountain town of Pale. As a Greek Orthodox Christian, he had reached out to fellow Orthodox countries and publicly stated, "The Bosnian Serbs have only two friends: God, and the Greeks." This was a fairly accurate statement at the time we received his letter.

Earlier that same year, The Carter Center and I had been accused of being excessively intrusive and independent in going to North Korea and Haiti, and I was determined to be very careful not to become involved with the

Serbs without approval from both the White House and the State Department. I immediately called President Bill Clinton, who encouraged my meeting with Karadžić's emissaries and asked that I give him a report immediately.

Within a few days, former ambassador Harry Barnes, director of our conflict resolution program, and Dr. Joyce Neu, associate director, brought Slavko Lazaraević and Dr. Djordjević to our home in Plains, and they explained that the Contact Group was refusing to deal with the Bosnian Serbs and communicating only with Milošević in Belgrade. The U.S. State Department had the same policy. There were excellent telephone communications, and the men spoke often with Karadžić during our meeting. They said he would make the necessary peace concessions directly to me if I would come to Pale and Sarajevo to talk to him and to the Bosnian Muslims personally. His representatives got him on the phone, and Karadžić pledged to me that he would do the following:

a. Permit normal movement of all UN relief convoys throughout Bosnia;
b. Remove any existing restraints on the free movement of representatives of the

United Nations;

c. Release all Muslim prisoners of war who were aged nineteen years or younger. He resisted total releases because he needed assurance that Bosnian Serb captives would be freed by the Bosnian Muslim authorities;

d. Honor a cease-fire around Sarajevo, which he did not control, and open the airport, which was controlled (or under attack) by his forces;

e. Guarantee human rights both now and in the future.

He assured me that all of these things would be announced within three hours and would be implemented within a day. I understood that these were major concessions demanded by the Contact Group, so I informed Karadžić that I would notify President Clinton. I did so while the Serb emissaries were still in Plains. Clinton was pleased but somewhat skeptical. I informed him that I would go to Sarajevo and Pale only if Karadžić first implemented his promises to me. We informed UN Secretary-General Boutros Boutros-Ghali and carried out an agreement with Karadžić that I also inform CNN, so that he could repeat his commitments and reveal his planned actions to their reporters in Bosnia.

That evening, Judy Woodruff interviewed Karadžić live on CNN, and he repeated the promises he had made to me, stating that the Serbs just needed someone who was trustworthy to communicate with them. I called the State Department and informed them about my tentative plans and said that if promises were kept I would go to the region without political status, representing only The Carter Center.

National Security Adviser Sandy Berger and Assistant Secretary of State Peter Tarnoff called and asked me about two additional points I had discussed with Karadžić and mentioned to the president: a comprehensive cease-fire and acceptance of the Contact Group's plan as a basis for negotiations. I explained that this was not to be announced in advance but that Karadžić would confirm it when I arrived in Bosnia. I mentioned the need for transportation from some major airport in Europe through Zagreb to Sarajevo and outlined my tentative schedule. They approved this request, but it was clear to me that White House officials were being careful to distance themselves from my involvement and that the United Nations was much more supportive.

Secretary of State Warren Christopher

called and suggested that I meet with Bosnian government leaders first and reminded me that the critical issue would be a cease-fire. Bosnian Muslims did not want a permanent cease-fire, which would freeze the present territorial gains of the Serbs, and they had offered three to four months maximum. Christopher suggested that if I could get Karadžić to accept the Contact Group proposal as a basis for negotiation and implement a cease-fire, I should let State, not The Carter Center, do the subsequent negotiation. I had no objection to this.

Once our trip was publicized, we were inundated with advice. French Foreign Minister Alain Juppé said that Karadžić's commitments to me were an "unacceptable provocation." He insisted that I should refer only to the Muslims as representing the Bosnian people. Democratic Senator Patrick Leahy of Vermont asked me not to promise anyone immunity from war-crimes trials. The Greek American Chris Spiro called from New Hampshire to say that nothing could be done in the Balkans without Milošević's approval; that Karadžić and Milošević were irreconcilable; and that Milošević controlled the borders, the military, space, and communications, and could have peace within two months while Karadžić would not survive six months. He said that Milošević wanted to meet with me, and I replied that I planned to meet with both Milošević and Karadžić and that the White House knew this.

The UN assistant secretary-general (later secretary-general) Kofi Annan called to welcome my trip, wish me well, and offer me full support. Lawrence Eagleburger, secretary of state under George H. W. Bush, attacked the Bosnia effort, as he had my visits to North Korea and Haiti, and stated that I was a floundering former president looking for publicity who hardly knew where Yugoslavia was located.

Before leaving home, I assessed all the information and advice and prepared a draft agreement that I hoped to consummate after meeting with Milošević, Karadžić, leaders of the Muslim Bosnians (Bozniaks), and representatives of the Contact Group.

With support from the White House, the State Department, and the United Nations, we went first to Frankfurt and then to Zagreb, where we met with the prime minister of Bosnia and the president of Croatia. Then we traveled to Sarajevo for a meeting with Alija Izetbegović, officially the president of Bosnia-Herzegovina. He was skeptical about our mission and had some fairly harsh demands, but none that deviated substantively from the prepared text I had in my pocket.

After a brief tour of war-ravaged Sarajevo, we drove to Pale. Because the direct road was mined, our route was circuitous (a seventy-five-minute drive to travel nine miles), through beautiful and undamaged farms, pastures, and mountain slopes reminiscent of the Alps. Realizing that Karadžić would have to obtain approval from the military leaders, I was glad that Ratko Mladić and other top generals and political leaders were present. Then Karadžić and his wife (also a psychiatrist) joined Rosalynn and me in a small room, with our peace fellow Harry Barnes coming in on occasion.

I presented my written proposal and we had a thorough discussion of all points. I was obdurate against any substantive changes but added a few things like "equal treatment of both sides" and "discussion of all issues." I reminded Karadžić that no one had seen this document except him, and that he was negotiating with me only. However, I had to be fair and open to both sides. I had only two days on this mission, not six months, and couldn't go back and forth between Pale and Sarajevo. He insisted that the Serbs must have a long cease-fire, and I responded that this was a change that neither Izetbegović nor the Contact Group would accept and my visit would be wasted if he would not concede on this point.

I threatened to leave if we couldn't reach agreement and brought him down from twelve to five months, and later to four. Karadžić wanted a private memorandum of understanding with me, and I replied that everything would have to be published and known by all concerned. After another argument, I threw in a promise to discuss all the proposed issues with Milošević, and that was enough.

Back in Sarajevo, I did most of my negotiating with Vice President Ejup Ganić, especially regarding prior acceptance of the Contact Group's recommendations. In fact, for the next five years, the design of a sentence that included the word *accept* would be the most intransigent issue. I liked Ganić, who was direct and forceful, and seemed to be thoughtful. After a tough discussion, I finally said I would not argue anymore. I was going back to Pale, and if Karadžić would agree to a cease-fire, I would announce that he had accepted the peace proposal and the Bosnia-Herzegovina government had refused. There was a Serb member of the government present who said, "You should be negotiating between the Contact Group and Karadžić, not us. We have accepted the Contact Group plan. It is not fair for you to put pressure on us." I emphasized that my language accepted by the Serbs was the same as that used by the Contact Group and the U.S. government. The Muslims were alone in their insistence on *accept* in advance of talks. At the end, Ganić said, "I'll think about your language overnight."

A mortar round had fallen in Sarajevo the previous evening, and I finally got a radio connection with Karadžić and demanded that the cease-fire be immediate and include all areas. He promised to respond the next morning, and President Izetbegović agreed and signed the two-page document that I had typed with the few changes demanded by Ganić. In summary, it committed Bosnia-Herzegovina to these provisions:

1. An immediate cease-fire, monitored by UN forces, and the exchange of prisoners will take place.
2. The parties will commence negotiations on a total cessation of hostilities, on December 27, 1994, to conclude by January 15, 1995. This cease-fire is to last for four months, or longer if mutually agreed.

3. During the cease-fire, the parties will negotiate a comprehensive peace agreement, with the Contact Group plan as a starting point.
4. Unrestricted movement of relief convoys with humanitarian services, using the airport at Sarajevo, will be permitted.
5. Each side will eliminate and prevent the firing of any guns or weapons that might be damaging to people or property.
6. Human rights will be protected in accordance with international standards. International human rights *rapporteurs* will be free to observe in all areas.
7. All detainees will be exchanged, under the auspices of the International Red Cross.
8. All items have to be agreed, or none are agreed.
9. Any other issues will be resolved utilizing the Contact Group or UN representatives.

This agreement was signed December 20, 1994, by Alija Izetbegović, witnessed by me.

Then we went back to Pale, where I finally accepted two improvements:

1. The cease-fire will commence at noon on December 23, 1994, monitored by UN forces, with the intent to conclude the agreement by January 1, 1995.
2. Based on assurances that convoys and humanitarian services will pass freely, the Bosnian forces will withdraw from the demilitarized zones before commencement of the negotiations described in item 1.

This agreement was signed December 21 by Ragovan Karadžić, witnessed by me.

My work was almost over, and when I arrived at the airport I obtained approval of the two changes from President Izetbegović before announcing them to the assembled news media and walking to our plane, guarded by a huge UN truck that shielded us from possible firing. Since the cease-fire had not commenced, we took off with our flak jackets on, knowing that the previous plane had taken four bullets through its left side. I took the hard drive out of my computer and put it and the signed documents inside my flak jacket.

It was snowing heavily in Zagreb, and we gave a brief report to UN Envoy Yasushi Akashi, then flew to Belgrade, where the weather was good. We were met with enthusiasm by Slobodan Milošević, who was accompanied every minute by Chris Spiro. We were served a banquet in the president's private office, sitting around a little coffee table. As did all the other leaders from the region, Milošević had to give me the history lesson first, but Rosalynn and I were thankful that he began with World War I instead of the twelfth century. I asked him repeatedly what it would take for him to restore relations with Karadžić, and he finally said that if his parliament voted for the "Carter Plan," this would be adequate.

I called Secretary of State Christopher to give him a report. He thanked me and promised that the U.S. government would be resolute in implementing all the agreements. Finally, on the way home from Frankfurt on a Delta Air Lines plane, we were annoyed when some last-minute duty-free Christmas presents were delivered to us in a Marlboro bag. I wrote Delta's CEO to complain about the airline's advertising cigarettes and urged him to ban all smoking on their flights.

I received an urgent message from Yasushi Akashi the next morning, reporting that the cease-fire had been negotiated, everything was quiet, and a provision called for any violations to be publicized, not concealed. It was signed by Izetbegović, Karadžić,

Bosnian General Derić, and Serbian General Ratko Mladić. The State Department called to say that the cease-fire was working "better than we had hoped" and the implementation agreement would be signed on December 30.

Under pressure from the Russians and some Europeans, the Contact Group still refused to meet with any Bosnian Serbs, having all their eggs in the Milošević basket. We had provided only four months to negotiate a permanent peace agreement, and they were stalemated on this point. I sent Milošević a letter urging him to advise the Contact Group to deal with Karadžić if and when the Serb parliament approved the peace deal.

The cease-fire held for five months instead of four, but the Contact Group frittered away the time, refusing to meet with the Bosnian Serbs, who offered to go to Geneva and negotiate on the basis of the Contact Group plan, as clarified by our agreement.

The situation deteriorated rapidly, and I finally decided in June 1995 to accept an invitation from Senator Sam Nunn to testify before a Senate committee about the stalemate. He said that General John Galvin, former supreme allied commander, Europe, and commander-in-chief of the U.S. European Command, agreed with me and would also testify. At the Senate, Nunn pointed out that I was the fifth president ever to testify, Truman having been the most recent. No Democrat or Republican disagreed with our basic premise: that peace talks between Bosnian Serbs and Muslim Croats should be exhausted before any military action was taken. I went by the White House to share our views with National Security Adviser Anthony Lake.

Sweden's former prime minister Carl Bildt called to tell me that he represented the European Union and agreed with our proposals involving the Bosnian Serbs but that the Contact Group would stick with Milošević for a short time. Secretary-General Boutros-Ghali told me that he agreed completely with my testimony and would try to shift attention to peace talks including the Bosnian Serbs.

We at The Carter Center urged the Bosnian Serb leadership to comply with UN demands to prevent the use of weapons against Sarajevo. At the same time, we attempted to find a way to assure that the Serb areas would not be attacked by Muslim Croat forces if all heavy weapons were removed. My suggestion was that the United States or NATO guarantee that these Bosnian promises would be honored if the Serbs would remove "a significant number" of their heavy weapons and let the remaining ones be placed under observation by UN forces.

In late August, Carl Bildt sent me a copy of their latest proposals, which was what we had been trying to get since December, including a nine-month lifting of sanctions against Yugoslavia to test Milošević's good faith. However, that same morning Croatia launched what seemed to be a war against the Serbs in the south, a Serbian shell fell on a market in Sarajevo, and NATO forces began a tremendous bombing of Serbian sites. Assistant Secretary of State Richard Holbrooke was in Belgrade, seeking some end to the conflict and using The Carter Center as an avenue to the Bosnian Serbs, when he was informed that Karadžić had agreed to let Milošević speak for all Serbs.

Finally, in November 1995, the parties agreed to meet in Dayton, Ohio, to negotiate a peace treaty under the supervision of the United States. The Croats and Serbs were left out of the negotiations, with their interests represented by Croatia's president Franjo Tudjman and Serbia's president, respectively. Alija Izetbegović represented the Bosnian government. The conference was chaired by Richard Holbrooke, with European Union Special Representative Carl Bildt and First Deputy Foreign Minister of Russia Igor Ivanov as co-chairmen.

As this agreement brought a temporary end to the war in Bosnia, Milošević was credited in the West with being one of the pillars of Balkan peace. The Dayton Agreement did not grant amnesty for the war crimes committed during the conflict.

A contingent of Albanians formed an armed force and contested control by Milošević of portions of Yugoslavia. Although the Serbian response was at first fairly restrained, by mid 1999 hundreds had died in escalating retaliations, and more than 100,000 Kosovo Albanians were reported to have been forced from their homes. The conflict culminated in the Kosovo War, which began in March 1999, with seventy-eight days of bombing by the air forces of the United States and NATO's other member nations. They flew over 36,000 sorties, and the Serbs were hit by more than 400 cruise missiles and 23,000 bombs, including cluster bombs and highly toxic depleted uranium bombs. This bombardment caused terrible destruction and eventually forced Milošević to back down.

Within three weeks, more than 800,000 Albanians had returned home, but about 250,000 Serbs, Bosniaks, and Gypsies fled to avoid revenge from the Albanians. To preserve the fragile peace, NATO now maintains a peacekeeping force of 45,000 troops in Kosovo.

It is interesting to conjecture about how many human rights atrocities, refugees, and deaths might have been avoided if our agreements and suggestions had been honored by the international community.

CUBA

One of our nation's most ill-advised and counterproductive policies is the prohibition against Americans' visiting Cuba and the punitive embargo against our 11 million neighbors who live under the communist regime of Fidel Castro. In more recent years, the intense animosity toward Cuba has also distorted our diplomatic relations with other Latin American countries.

Under the George W. Bush administration, top officials in the State Department and National Security Council seem to be chosen to deal with issues in this region only after they have been proven to be publicly and persistently rabid in their expressions of hatred for Castro. Gross distortions of the "threats against our security" have been used to justify the separation of our two nations (only ninety miles apart) and to undermine Castro's regime by making his oppressed subjects suffer economically. A majority of the U.S. Congress agrees that travel restraints and trade sanctions should be eased or lifted entirely, but promises of a presidential veto have stymied legislative desires.

As a new president in 1977, I lifted all travel limitations between our two countries, believing that the best avenue to more freedom and democracy in Cuba was to expose its citizens to tourists, family members, business and professional leaders seeking opportunities for trade and commerce, and athletes desiring to compete. We took the first step in political communication by establishing "interest sections" in Washington and Havana, with a goal of full diplomatic relations. Unfortunately, the involvement of Cuban troops in African trouble spots and a massive "boatlift" of refugees to America's shores delayed further progress, and my successors in office have reinstituted and tightened the restraints.

In 1989 I represented The Carter Center at the inauguration of Carlos Andrés Pérez as president of Venezuela, and while there I had a brief private conversation with Fidel Castro. Perhaps surprisingly, our discussion concentrated on health care in the developing world. The Center was rapidly expanding our fight against preventable tropical diseases, and we were finding a number of Cuban doctors in the most remote areas in Africa and Latin America. They were living among the poorest people and receiving only small stipends for their work. We didn't really have time to explore any specific opportunities for cooperation, but we later had a chance to discuss the subject more thoroughly when we met again.

During the following years, The Carter Center pursued a number of avenues to better understand the relationship between the United States and Cuba, meeting with Cuban American leaders from Miami who represented a wide range of opinion about dealing with Castro. There was a crisis in August 1994, when Castro permitted thousands of Cubans to form a boatlift to Florida, very similar to what had happened while I was president. Recalling the Mariel Boatlift crisis of 1980, when rioting Cubans in Arkansas damaged him politically, President Bill Clinton now vowed there would be no dialogue or communication with Cuba and began transferring Cuban boat people to Guantánamo. Castro responded by lifting all restraints on Cuban émigrés, and the number intercepted at sea rose to almost three thousand.

At this point, on August 23, some moderate Cuban Americans asked me if The Carter Center would act as mediator between Castro and Clinton, and I responded that we would do so only if there was no alternative and that my role would remain secret but approved in advance by both governments. Within twenty-four hours I had these assurances, both from the U.S. State Department and from Castro. I was asked to deal only with Peter Tarnoff, undersecretary of state for political affairs. The key issue was whether the United States would have direct talks with Cuba on a number of issues (not just immigration), would honor previous commitments on a legal immigration quota of more than twenty thousand annually, and would permit some Cubans incarcerated at Guantánamo to return to Cuba if they desired to do so. I received a copy of a message from Tarnoff to Castro that was somewhat equivocal about Cuba's demands but relayed the response to Castro.

The next day a storm was developing in the Caribbean, with predicted seven-foot waves that would endanger thousands of Cubans in open boats. I decided to call President Clinton to expedite the process and clarify the U.S. position. I outlined what

I considered to be minimum concessions and offered to withdraw my involvement or to continue with his personal approval. However, I needed some flexibility in dealing with Castro. The president promised a quick response, and I soon received a call from Tarnoff affirming Clinton's desire for me to continue my effort.

Emphasizing that I was representing The Carter Center and not acting officially, I submitted a proposal during the evening of August 26 to Fernando Ramírez, Cuban ambassador to the United Nations, to be transmitted to Castro. It recommended that talks begin the following week in Washington or New York, that the agenda extend beyond immigration, that the outflow of boat people be stopped, that the U.S. immigration quota be raised to 28,000 annually, and that Cubans in Guantánamo desiring to return to Cuba could do so and not be punished. The next day, Ramírez informed me that Castro would call me at my home that evening.

When the Cuban leader called, he and I recalled our meeting in Venezuela, and then he asked me to repeat the terms I had suggested to Minister Ramírez. Castro tried to justify his decision to open "one thousand miles of coastline" to boat people but said he would send high-level officials to New York on Wednesday to negotiate in good faith on the basis I had suggested. He wanted me to stay involved, but I told him I had to leave for Africa the following day and wanted to complete arrangements before my departure. I reported this conversation to the State Department, and the next day I had a call from Vice President Al Gore, who expressed thanks for what had been accomplished, said that an alternative communication channel had been established, and asked that I refrain from further participation. I told him I was leaving that night for Africa but would summarize the terms for U.S.-Cuba talks to Tarnoff and Castro. After visiting Mauritania and Ivory Coast, and arriving in Liberia, I was informed by the U.S. ambassador that the talks in New York had been successful.

We were hopeful that there would be an easing of tension between Cuba and America, but we underestimated the influence of Senator Jesse Helms of North Carolina, who had become chairman of the Senate Foreign Relations Committee. He was finally able to realize a longtime ambition of tightening restraints on Cuba in 1996, by inducing the Congress to pass legislation that strengthened the U.S. embargo against Cuba, extended it to foreign companies trading with Cuba, and penalized foreign companies allegedly "trafficking" in Cuban property formerly owned by Cubans who have since become U.S. citizens. Surprisingly, President Clinton signed the bill into law, thus moving the embargo from presidential to congressional control.

Although we tried to arrange several meetings with some top Cuban officials, the U.S. State Department always managed to subvert these sessions by denying visas to key people, and Castro reacted by not letting anyone participate. Now under much more difficult circumstances, The Carter Center continued to investigate possibilities of easing opposition from Cuban American groups, and we had a series of sessions in Atlanta in 2003 and 2004 with about twenty people at a time representing a broad range of attitudes. They made it clear that these meetings offered a rare opportunity for them to talk to one another, and we learned a lot from them.

My next encounter with Fidel Castro came in October 2000, when my close friend Canadian Prime Minister Pierre Trudeau died and I went to his memorial service in Montreal. It happened that I was the senior person in the U.S. delegation, Castro led the Cubans, and he and I were at the head of the honorary funeral procession. We stood alone for more than a half hour as the protocol officers arranged other dignitaries in line. We had a cordial conversation, in which he recalled our previous encounters, expressed admiration for the health work of The Carter Center in the Third World, and told me that he had a large number of medical doctors deployed in many of the same countries. He wanted me to come to Cuba to discuss how we might cooperate, and I told him I would need an official invitation, which he promised to send.

This began a long series of quiet negotiations between us, as I insisted on unlimited contact with the Cuban people during my visit, and his responses were mostly about national laws, practical problems with access to media, and generalities about constitutionally guaranteed freedoms of speech and movement. I insisted, and Castro finally sent me word that I could speak directly to the entire population on television. There was then the question of whether I should speak from the central square of Havana or in a more academic setting. I chose the University of Havana, with my remarks to be followed by questions from the students and faculty.

The next step was to notify the U.S. State Department that our group from The Carter

Center would be making the trip under authorization as an educational institution. We applied for a Treasury Department license to travel, as required for any other Americans. Before the trip, we had a number of briefings from interested groups, including the conservative Cuban American National Foundation, academic experts, international agencies, the U.S. State Department, and intelligence agencies.

I let them know that our goals were to establish a frank dialogue with President Castro, to communicate directly with the Cuban people, and to pursue ways to improve U.S.-Cuban relations. I wanted to explore with the president and other Cuban leaders any signs of flexibility in economic or political policy that might help to ease tensions between our two countries. I thought the example of Deng Xiaoping's transformation of China's economy by gradually permitting the expansion of small family businesses might be one possibility.

The Varela Project was a subject of great publicity in the United States (and none in Cuba). It had been started by democracy activists in 1998, was led by Oswaldo Payá of the Christian Liberation Movement, and bore the name of Félix Varela, an eighteenth-century Catholic priest. As per-

President and Mrs. Carter enjoyed a warm welcome from Cuban citizens during a walking tour of historic Old Havana during their trip to Cuba in May 2002. (ANNEMARIE POYO)

mitted under Cuba's constitution, a petition from ten thousand citizens to change Cuban laws would be considered by the National Assembly. Such a petition from more than eleven thousand citizens was presented a few days before our arrival. It called for a referendum on five points: (1) freedom of expression and association; (2) amnesty for political prisoners not accused of attempted murder; (3) rights of private enterprise; (4) direct election of public officials; and (5) elections to be held within one year. In my speech to the nation, I planned to call for some of these rights, as well as the establishment of a blue-ribbon commission to resolve property claims, an extensive exchange of university students with the United States, international inspectors to investigate prisons and human rights abuses, and the utilization of responsible Cuban Americans as a possible bridge between Cuba and the United States.

A day or so before we left, we received a schedule from Havana for me to speak at 3:00 P.M., when most people would be at work, but they finally agreed to change the time to 6:30 and to provide full television coverage. It still concerned us that there was no mention of radio. I decided to speak in Spanish to avoid any possibility of manipulation of the translation.

Rosalynn and I had no idea what to expect, but we were received at the Havana airport with full honors and a warm welcoming address by Castro. We considered it significant that he wore a business suit rather than his normal military uniform. I responded in Spanish, giving the time and place of my major speech and expressing hope that it could be broadcast through both television and radio. (In fact, it was advertised in *Granma,* the official newspaper.)

During our ride to the hotel, Castro assured me that there would be no restraints on my movements or contacts with dissidents or religious leaders, that all my activities and statements would be covered by the large foreign news media contingent, and that my Tuesday speech would be carried live on television and radio and rebroadcast at later times.

That evening President Castro and I had a general discussion, and then we enjoyed an informal supper, attended by our group and Vice President Carlos Lage, National Assembly President Ricardo Alarcón, Foreign Minister Felipe Pérez Roque, and a few other officials. Castro often keeps foreign visitors up all night, but he respected our desire for sleep and abbreviated his remarks. He couldn't resist giving us detailed information about Cuban achievements in science, agriculture, health, and education. From then on, he was careful to end Rosalynn's and my participation in each night's activities at midnight but frequently remained until much later with the other guests.

We managed to concentrate on a few key issues, including those that would be included in my speech, such as the Varela Project, release of political prisoners, permission for families to have small businesses and hire neighbors, an invitation to the International Red Cross and the UN High Commissioner for Human Rights to visit the country and ascertain the status of prisons and human rights, and graduate student exchanges. Castro took notes, said he would consider all the issues, and offered to make fifty Cuban doctors available to help with The Carter Center's African health projects. He stated that Cuba was already sending more than 2,750 doctors to serve in poorer countries.

The next morning we met with Oswaldo Payá, leader of the Varela Project, and Elizardo Sánchez, Cuba's best-known human rights leader. Payá explained the process of having secured more than eleven thousand signatures on the petition, assured us that the U.S. government had not given assistance to the effort, and stated that he would have refused such help. I described the responses I had received during the previous evening's banquet from Cuban officials, which were legally technical and attempted to distinguish between changes in laws versus constitutional amendments.

We then went to the medical research and pharmaceutical center and received a detailed report on some of Cuba's extraordinary progress in research on and treatment of Alzheimer's, hepatitis B and C, some forms of cancer, and meningitis. Cuban pharmaceutical manufacturers were sharing technology with several nations and a number of international pharmaceutical companies, with tight constraints against use for illicit purposes. Perhaps timed to disrupt our visit to Cuba, U.S. Undersecretary of State for Arms Control and International Security John Bolton made the following statement:

We know that Cuba is collaborating with other state sponsors of terror.... Analysts and Cuban defectors have long cast suspicion on the activities conducted in these biomedical facilities. Here is what we now know: The United States believes that Cuba has at least a limited offensive biological warfare research and development effort. Cuba has provided dual-use biotechnology to other rogue states. We are concerned that such technology could support biological weaons programs in those states. We call on Cuba to cease all BW-applicable cooperation with rogue states and to fully comply with all of its obligations under the Biological Weapons Convention.

When we repeated Bolton's allegations to the Cuban scientists, they laughed and said he was a source of many lies. They authorized me to invite a team of scientific investigators from the United States, who would be given a free hand to inspect any of their facilities. I made this invitation public, but there was no response from Washington. I had previously been told by U.S. intelligence officials that Cuba did not pose any threat regarding biological weapons.

During our remaining days in Cuba, we had extensive meetings with their top officials and with diplomatic representatives from other countries and the United Nations. They helped us develop an itinerary and schedule that would engage Cuban society most effectively and permit us to make visits with only brief prior notice to our hosts. One interesting school was for high school graduates who did not meet the standards for the university and were given two years of college-level education as they provided social services to needy people. We also witnessed a remarkable performance in dance, music, and drama by mentally retarded and handicapped children, many with Down syndrome.

One of our most interesting visits was to a remarkable medical school where I was invited to address the six thousand students, assembled between our speaking platform and the sea. Here, with all expenses paid, young people were receiving six years of education and then being prepared to pass the examinations to practice medicine in their own countries. None of them were from Cuba; they had come from a number of African countries, twenty-three Latin American nations, and even the United States. The thirty-one American students had completed their first year, including Spanish-language training, and told us that their only cost was for airplane tickets when they returned home for a visit.

World Health Organization officials told us that Cuba had had great success in controlling AIDS. Each infected patient was given intensive medical care and counseling, and every pregnant woman was tested for HIV/AIDS. If found to be HIV positive, she received complete treatment with AZT (produced in Cuba). The organization's statistics showed that the incidence of AIDS in Cuba was the lowest in this hemisphere, with only one HIV-positive baby born the previous year. More than eight hundred Cuban doctors were in Haiti working to control the AIDS epidemic there.

As a farmer, I was interested in agricultural cooperatives. We had time to visit only one of them, with 151 families working about 700 acres of land. They were producing a wide variety of grain, vegetables, fruits, and flowers. The elected leader of the co-op made an unusually large annual salary, the equivalent of twelve hundred U.S. dollars. (Most people earned about six U.S. dollars per month, but their earnings had high value in buying food, medicine, clothing, and housing.) They pointed out that there was a high degree of private enterprise in the marketing of agricultural products and that city families had recently been encouraged to plant small garden plots around their homes and sell their excess produce. This was one of the few opportunities for self-employment permitted, in addition to motor transport, small restaurants, the renting of rooms in one's own house, and repair work in the homes of others.

We visited a housing development similar to a Habitat for Humanity project, with families obtaining titles to their homes by making monthly payments of forty pesos, equivalent to U.S. $1.50. Not even Castro's enemies questioned the fact that 85 percent of Cubans owned their own homes or that practically 100 percent of the people were literate, were immunized against all childhood diseases, and had family physician care.

Tuesday evening, at the University of Havana, I made my speech in Spanish and then answered questions from the students and faculty. I glanced a few times at President Castro sitting in the front row and never detected any change in his demeanor, even during my most critical comments regarding human rights abuses in Cuba. As promised, all this was carried live on television and radio, and was later rebroadcast several times, and (to my surprise) the entire transcript was published in the two Cuban newspapers. Subsequently, we could not find anyone on the streets or in the markets who had not heard it, and many people showed us the news copies they were carrying. All analysts said it was the first time in forty-three years that citizens had heard any public criticism of the Cuban government, much less direct condemnation of human rights violations, a call for international inspectors, and promotion of the Varela Project.

President Castro greeted me after the session and reminded me that it was time for us to attend the Cuban all-star baseball game. In Cuba, baseball is the preeminent sport, combining the popularity in other nations of basketball, football, cricket, and soccer. He and I rode in different cars, and when we arrived at the stadium, we both entered the dugout area.

He stopped, turned to me, and said, "Mr. President, I have a special request to make. It will be my only one during your visit."

I replied, "Certainly, President Castro. What is it?"

He said, "I would like for you and me to walk to the pitcher's mound without any of my security officers or your Secret Service."

I glanced at Agent in Charge Rick Kerr; he had no objection, so I gave Castro a nod.

Predictably, the stadium was packed, and everyone cheered as we walked to the center of the field. Having been asked earlier to throw out the first ball, I had practiced pitching from the proper distance and threw one ball to home plate, then another. Finally, after we were seated in the stadium, I signed both balls, and Castro did the same. Each of us took one, and later he gave his ball to Rick Kerr. My ball was later auctioned for the benefit of The Carter Center and aroused spirited bidding from all over the nation, with a final price of $175,000. Several people suggested that I go to Cuba each year, just to throw out the first ball. (Rick also gave his ball to The Carter Center, and it brought in almost as much.)

One of our most interesting discussions was with National Assembly President Ricardo Alarcón, who had just received the Varela petition. He told us in rather roundabout language that the government had not yet decided how to respond, but he saw both a technical issue based on interpretation of the law and a political issue. Legally, he said, the petition could be peremptorily rejected, but politically it would be necessary to justify a decision to the people. He claimed that it was just a "North American" project, and I tried to convince him that it came from Cubans and that the petitioners deserved a full and open hearing, even if their effort was to be rejected.

Apparently, there is freedom of worship in Cuba provided there are no criticisms of the government from the pulpit. We went to

After throwing the first pitch, President Carter joined President Fidel Castro in the stands for a baseball game. (ANNEMARIE POYO)

the Martin Luther King Center for an assembly of Jews and Protestant Christians. After songs and the main sermon, mostly concerning the suffering caused by the U.S. embargo, I was asked to give an impromptu message in Spanish. This group seemed fervent in their faith but almost totally aligned with Cuban policy and when questioned could think of no real criticisms or desired changes in government policies. They did ask for more access to mass media, publishing materials, and new church buildings, and realized that they had to be more closely united with Christians in other nations. We met separately with Catholic leaders, who were grateful for permission to hold religious services and not to be outlawed completely, and cautious about any public challenge to the government on controversial issues.

One evening Rosalynn and I met privately for almost two hours with Castro, one aide, and his interpreter; I pressed him unsuccessfully on some suggestions for opening up his closed political and economic system and other points covered in my university speech. We later assessed his motivations as belief in equity of treatment among Cuban citizens, but also a determination to retain the tightest possible control over all aspects of life that might cause criticism or threaten his regime. Also, he feared that any conciliatory action would be seen as a sign of weakness in his long political battle with the United States. After our private meeting, we attended a large and ornate official banquet, where the courses were interspersed with delightful musical entertainment. We noticed here and in many other musical performances the dominance of John Lennon's song "Imagine," played in different ways.

One morning we drove about seventy-five miles to the Pinar del Río province for bird-watching, followed by unannounced visits to villages and public places. In one typical small city of about 20,000, there were three health clinics and one hospital, with a doctor for each 170 people (the national average). There were some shortages of medicine and an EKG machine with the wrong kind of paper, but the staff said that they could deliver preventive medical services as well as give family care and emergency treatment, and that the EKG in the hospital worked properly.

At a large farmers' market, we visited some of the seven hundred booths that were rented to private entrepreneurs for 5 percent of their sales. There was a wide assortment of prepared foods, vegetables, fruits, and meats. The shopkeepers said they bought

their produce directly from farm cooperatives or *campesinos,* and their businesses
were thriving. The place was packed with
customers, except for a small section devoted to sales by the government, which attracted few people. Our final day included
a tour through Ernest Hemingway's home
and a concert of classical music and dance,
modern Cuban music, and folklore. At the
end, all of us joined the performers on the
outdoor stage and continued dancing.

Although we were sure that we were observed by government agents, we had extensive meetings with twenty-seven of the
most notable human rights dissidents. Each
was the leader of an organization, and many
had served prison sentences for their public criticisms of government policies. They
were unanimous in expressing appreciation
for my speech, in their willingness to risk
punishment rather than be silent, in their
opposition to further harsh rhetoric from the
United States toward Cuba, in their hope that
American visitation could be expanded, and
in their refusal of direct or indirect funding
of their efforts by the U.S. government. Any
knowledge or report of such financial support would confirm Castro's long-standing
claims that they were "paid lackeys" of
Washington. Although some doubted the

effectiveness of the Varela Project, all except one of the dissidents agreed that their organizations should support it.

I had a press conference before leaving Havana, at which I summarized my thoughts about issues and our experiences in Cuba, and on the way home I prepared a full trip report and sent it to the White House and State Department. A few days later I went to Washington to share my thoughts and answer questions with about a hundred congressional leaders and then had a pleasant private session with President George W. Bush and Condoleezza Rice.

Almost immediately, it was announced from the White House that U.S. policies regarding Cuba would be more restrictive and punitive and that a veto awaited any legal expression of the known desire of majorities in the House and Senate to ease travel and economic restraints toward our neighbor. At The Carter Center, we decided to continue our efforts to bring freedom to Cuba and to encourage friendly relations between Americans and the Cuban people.

CHAPTER THREE
STRENGTHENING DEMOCRACY

PANAMA

I have often said that the most difficult political challenge I ever faced was to negotiate and have the U.S. Senate approve a new agreement with Panama concerning the canal and the zone it crosses. Every president since Dwight Eisenhower had faced increasingly serious arguments with the Panamanian people over sovereignty in the zone. It was mutually agreed in 1963 that no national flags would be flown in the area, but this pact was violated a few weeks later by some American students, and massive rioting had to be brought under control by U.S. troops. Four of our soldiers and at least twenty Panamanians were dead after three days of fighting, which led to the breaking of diplomatic relations between the two nations and a subsequent pledge by President Lyndon Johnson and Panamanian President Roberto Chiari to renegotiate the existing treaties.

Because of intense domestic political pressures, Presidents Lyndon Johnson, Richard Nixon, and Gerald Ford reneged on this promise, and the issue became a cause célèbre of the Latin American people and others in the developing world. I inherited the problem and was eventually able to negotiate two treaties that acknowledged Panama's sovereignty over the canal — the first to extend to the end of the year 2000 and a permanent one to follow. Panama was ruled at the time by Omar Torrijos, a military dictator, and he promised me that he would change the country to a democratic nation.

Torrijos was killed in an airplane crash six months after I left office and was succeeded by another military commander, Manuel Noriega. He was corrupt and ruled in such an illegal manner that the international community and his own citizens demanded democratic reforms. Self-deluded and surrounded by sycophants, he was convinced that his chosen candidates would easily prevail, and he scheduled elections for May 1989. Responding to pressure from the opposition, he finally agreed that there be an international observer team headed by President Gerald Ford and me. Noriega had worked closely with the Reagan administration in the American effort to overthrow the

Sandinista regime in Nicaragua by organizing and giving full support to a rebel force known as the Contras. When he shifted his allegiance to the Sandinistas, President Reagan banned all contacts with the Panamanian government.

By the time of the election, George H. W. Bush was president, and the "Contra War" was still being waged. The Center prescribed some fairly strict electoral procedures, which Noriega reluctantly implemented, and I received permission from Washington for The Carter Center to accept his invitation. In a joint effort with the National Democratic Institute and the International Republican Institute, we marshaled our first election monitoring team. Two days before the election, Rosalynn and I met with Noriega in his tightly protected military headquarters. We sat around a table, and I remember that his upper body was remarkably short, so that his badly pockmarked face was barely visible above the tabletop. He was not running for office himself but was putting forward his handpicked candidates for president and two vice presidents, and it was obvious to us that he did not intend to relinquish political power. When I asked him repeatedly whether he would accept the results if they lost the election, he was not able to conceive of such a ridiculous possibility.

The Panamanians had a fairly accurate list of registered voters, the voting procedures were reasonable, and it seemed that a distinguished group of college presidents, prominent lawyers, and other civil leaders constituted the Election Commission. Also, the Catholic Church had decided to observe the final vote counts at a number of representative polling sites around the country to provide a rough indication of the results and to share them with us. We called this a "quick count." Noriega assured us that our observers could perform their duties without interference.

This was Panama's first experience with real democracy, and 800,000 citizens — about three-fourths of those on the approved list — poured out to vote on Election Day. It was obvious to our own monitors that Noriega's candidates were losing badly, and the quick count indicated that the margin was three to one. Shortly after midnight, I was informed that men in civilian clothes but carrying weapons were visiting many of the polling places and confiscating the ballots and vote tabulations. I left my hotel, visited several of the sites, and found the report to be accurate. Some organized bands of men, none in uniform, threw large rocks at my automobile as we drove down the streets.

The following morning I met with opposition candidates and spoke a number of times by phone with Noriega, trying to convince him to accept the loss and become a hero for having brought democracy to his country. He seemed equivocal for several hours but broke off contact shortly after noon. His soldiers had been quite friendly to me and our team, but now they barred me from entering the large auditorium where election results were being announced and posted on the walls. They finally let me enter, "to observe the announcement of the final results." The members of the "blue-ribbon" Election Commission were on a stage, and I pushed my way to the front of the crowd.

We had copies of a number of the genuine tally sheets, each one carefully filled out and signed by at least ten polling officials and party observers. The ones now being used were partial, containing only numbers in the totaled slots, and most with only two or three signatures, often in the same handwriting. Noriega's candidates were being announced as winners by a two-to-one margin. I was very angry and climbed onto the stage. In Spanish, I shouted, "Are you honest officials or thieves? You are stealing the election from the people of Panama." Soldiers forced me off the stage and ushered me to my hotel, which was across a broad street. I was informed that I could not return to the election headquarters, where dozens of local and international news reporters were assembled.

We finally decided to have a press conference in the hotel and I had some of my staff with press credentials inform the media representatives. I described what had happened to a large group of reporters, denounced the election process as fraudulent, and called on world leaders to unite in condemning it. We were able to make our way to the airport with some difficulty and returned home, and we were glad to see the Organization of American States condemn this violation of human rights, and the United States and several other countries impose economic sanctions on Panama. Noriega did not attempt to install his candidates, but he prevented the real winners from taking office by declaring the elections null and void.

When severe economic pressures failed to dislodge Noriega as military leader, President George H. W. Bush ordered U.S. troops to invade Panama late that year. The renegade commander was eventually arrested, but only after twenty-five Americans and more than a thousand Panamanians were killed and the nation was severely damaged by the combat. The Organization of American States and the UN General Assembly condemned the U.S. invasion as a "flagrant violation of international law," but many Panamanians approved the capture of Noriega when the honestly elected candidates took office. The Carter Center has monitored subsequent elections in the country.

As a matter of interest, Noriega was found guilty in a U.S. court and sentenced in September 1992 to forty years in prison for drug and racketeering violations. His sentence was later reduced to thirty years, and with good behavior he was scheduled to be freed in September 2007, but both the Panamanian and French governments have sought his extradition to face charges of murder and money laundering.

NICARAGUA

The United States has had a long and troubled relationship with Nicaragua. Early in the twentieth century, American troops occupied the country and controlled its political, military, and economic affairs for about twenty years. When we withdrew in 1933, Anastasio Somoza García became commandant of the military forces and soon anointed himself political dictator. When he died twenty years later, his son assumed this power and continued to enjoy a friendly and supportive relationship with Washington. In 1979, a large coalition of revolutionaries and political opponents was successful in overthrowing Somoza, and about a dozen of their leaders came to visit me in the White House. They promised to establish a democratic government and to rule in harmony with one another, but they soon divided into competing factions and the revolutionary Sandinistas became dominant. Their leader, Daniel Ortega, became president.

While I was visiting Ghana in 1989, soon after our having condemned the fraudulent election in Panama, I received a request from President Ortega for The Carter Center to monitor the Nicaraguan election scheduled for the following February. Ortega and the Sandinistas had prevailed in a 1984 contest that was approved by some observer groups but declared unacceptable by the Reagan administration, and I presumed that the Sandinistas were confident of another victory and wanted it to be internationally recognized.

At that time, Nicaragua was torn apart. Armed and equipped by the Reagan administration, a military group known as the Contras had been waging a ferocious war against the government since 1982. The armed conflict and an economic embargo by the United States had resulted in a fiscal crisis and the loss of 35,000 lives. We saw a fair election as a means of ending the war and healing the divisions within Nicaraguan society and reached out to others to join us. The United Nations agreed to monitor elections in a sovereign nation for the first time by declaring it an international security issue. The Organization of American States helped to mediate a cease-fire between the Contras and the Nicaraguan government, and also formed an election observer mission.

An international effort to demobilize the Contras was initiated, but fighting continued during the political campaign and election. Although the United States still refused communication with the Sandinista regime and the war continued, President George H. W. Bush and Secretary of State James Baker approved our involvement.

Under the direction of Carter Center fellow Dr. Robert Pastor, our team began to assess Nicaragua's election laws and procedures. The Nicaraguans devised new election laws, but some discrepancies remained. One challenge was the development of a complete and accurate list of qualified voters, and an excellent plan was evolved. During each weekend in October, the future polling sites were opened and the officials who were to conduct the election registered all citizens who wished to vote. It was an open process, the polling places became well known, and officials were acquainted with their neighbors who would later be voting. The only problem was that the Contra war was still being waged, with Nicaraguan Contra troops launching attacks from Honduras into the northern counties. The conflict interfered with voter registration in that region and would obstruct voting two months later.

We coordinated our mission with the United Nations and the OAS as observers. In the meantime, party alignments were being formed. With the country so divided, it was unlikely that the Sandinistas had support from a majority of the citizens, but the opposition was fragmented among more than a dozen competing parties and they were unable to agree on any notable candidate to represent them. Finally, however, fourteen of the parties formed an alliance, the National Opposition Union (UNO), and chose as their candidate Violeta Chamorro, a member of the original junta formed after the defeat of Somoza. She was editor of the anti-Somoza newspaper *La Prensa,* having succeeded her husband when he was assassinated in January 1978.

A number of crises threatened the electoral process, and one or two members of The Carter Center's Council of Freely Elected Heads of Government visited Nicaragua frequently to resolve disputes. I went myself four times and worked out agreements to allow the participation of Miskito Indians, to end campaign violence, and to ensure the delivery of legal foreign contributions to the UNO campaign. We required that both sides pledge not to make any preliminary claim of victory until the final results were promulgated by the Election Commission. Last-minute polling results were mixed, but the Sandinistas appeared to consider themselves invulnerable.

On Election Day, our observers were deployed throughout the country and reported that everything was going well — until noon. Bob Pastor, Rosalynn, and a small group were having lunch with me when I received a report that the indelible ink placed on voters' fingers to prevent their casting a second ballot had been found to wash off when rubbed with chlorine bleach. The word was spreading all over the country, and there were allegations that the election could be rigged. When we consulted with the Election Commission and met with the campaign chairmen of the major parties, we found that both of them were confident of victory and wanted to proceed without interruption.

After the polls closed, our observers went to assigned locations to witness the counting of ballots. The national television and radio stations began to give preliminary results but returned to programs of only music at about nine o'clock. An hour later, we received reports from the UN quick count indicating that the Sandinistas were losing by at least 12 percent. I urged the Election Commission to resume broadcasting up-to-date returns, but they refused. Since there were party observers at every polling place, they also knew what had happened.

Finally, at about midnight, Daniel Ortega called to request that I, along with the OAS and UN leaders, come to Sandinista headquarters to convince their leaders to accept the results peacefully. On the way we saw large crowds of supporters, with musicians ready to lead the celebration. They were quiet but increasingly restless, awaiting word of their victory. The Sandinista leaders, known as "Comandantes," were assembled behind a long table, and we were seated opposite them along with leaders of the UN and the OAS. I informed them bluntly that they had lost by a large margin and urged them to let the final tallies be broadcast. I reminded them that I had been defeated also but was enjoying a "second life," and that their party could continue to play an important role in Nicaraguan politics. I advised Ortega to make a statement early in the morning to take credit for the democratic election and achievements of the revolution while acknowledging his defeat. I also promised to try to persuade the U.S. government to control the Contra military forces so that there would be no attacks on the Sandinistas and said that I would remain in Nicaragua until these promises were assured. The leaders listened quietly, and Ortega finally nodded.

I jotted down an outline of what he might say, suggesting 6:00 A.M. as an appropriate time. We then went to see Mrs. Chamorro and asked her to urge her supporters to await the official results. She agreed, and I gave her some recommendations on a gracious victory statement to be made at the same time.

I returned to my hotel room and placed a call to Secretary Baker in Washington. It was four o'clock, and he answered sleepily but was overjoyed by the news. I urged him also to make a positive statement, not condemning the Sandinistas and at least giving them credit for conducting and accepting the results of an honest and fair election.

He asked, "What should I say?"

I asked, "Do you have a pencil?"

I dictated a few remarks, and he agreed to issue his statement simultaneously with those of Ortega and Chamorro.

Bob Pastor and I remained in Nicaragua for a few days to assure implementation of three major provisos: (1) The United States would assist UNO leaders in disarming the Contras before they were allowed to return from Honduras. (2) The Sandinista army would remain intact but would serve as the national military force, under the leadership of Ortega's brother but commanded by Mrs. Chamorro. (3) The revolutionary members would be allowed to retain a certain portion of the property confiscated from Somoza's supporters. We finally reached a reasonable agreement on these and other matters, and a carefully worded joint statement was issued before we returned home. It was almost unprecedented to see a revolutionary regime that came to power through armed struggle relinquish its power as a result of a free election.

Daniel Ortega and his associates continued to play an increasingly powerful role in government even though they lost the next two national elections. The Sandinistas finally prevailed in 2006, and Ortega became president in the fourth difficult Nicaraguan election that has been monitored by The Carter Center.

GUYANA

The most personal danger I have felt since leaving the White House was in Guyana in 1992. This small nation on the northern coast of South America was then and still is the most completely divided that I know. About 9 percent of its citizens are Amerindians living mostly in the vast forests, and another 80 percent are divided between descendants of indentured servants from India and descendants of African slaves, both brought in by the British during colonial times. The major political parties are largely separated along these racial lines, as are many of the basic professions.

The Indo-Guyanese hold a slight majority, but the Afro-Guyanese and their People's National Congress (PNC) party were able to control the government from the time of national independence in 1966, assisted by the government of Great Britain and the CIA, both of which considered Cheddi

Jagan, leader of the opposition People's Progressive Party (PPP), to be a Marxist.

In 1990, Mr. Jagan came to The Carter Center, claimed that previous elections had been fraudulent, and asked us to help ensure that the next one would be honest and fair. We agreed, provided the ruling party would also accept our presence as observers. For several months, President Desmond Hoyte objected strongly, but public opinion became so greatly aroused that he finally agreed, just one month before the election was scheduled. Bob Pastor and his team developed a list of minimal election standards, and I went to Guyana to discuss them with the president and others. Three of the most important were to have an accurate voters' list, a politically balanced election commission, and votes counted at the polling places.

These issues had been hotly debated for almost thirty years and were very difficult for the ruling party to accept. Finally, as I was preparing to leave the country and declare that we could not participate, President Hoyte accepted all of our provisions. The election was delayed until October 1992, and government officials also invited as observers of the British Commonwealth, with which they had enjoyed a close and friendly relationship.

As usual, we deployed our two-person teams throughout the country before Election Day, and I went west along the coast toward the border with Venezuela to visit a few polling sites in a riverine area inhabited by Arawak Indians, traveling from one village to another in a small boat. On the way back to Georgetown, the capital, we flew over the famous site of the 1978 mass suicide of Jim Jones and more than nine hundred of his cult followers. When we arrived at the airport, our small plane was surrounded by members of the security forces, who informed me that riots had broken out all over Georgetown and that I must go to the U.S. embassy, where I would be safe.

Instead, I went to my hotel room and called President Hoyte, who assured me that the police were in charge and order would soon be restored. Bob Pastor informed me that the PNC were obviously losing the election, and that some of their supporters had been induced to disrupt the process. I decided that the election should continue if possible and sent word to our observers to monitor events and, after the polls closed, to go to their assigned places to gather quick count results. Our senior observer, Jennifer McCoy, told me that the election center had come under attack by an angry mob, some of whom claimed to have been denied a ballot. She had visited the building and tried to work out a solution with the PNC party chief, but the riot continued.

The election center was where all of the communication equipment and computers, on which election results would be tabulated, were located. It was a two-story wooden building with many windows, with the electronic equipment housed in an isolated central room on the second floor. When I arrived, accompanied by three Secret Service agents, the building was surrounded by several hundred rioters, who had already broken all the windows with clubs and stones. There was only one Guyanese police officer present, a woman wearing a uniform but without sidearms.

We went upstairs and found that all the computers had been transferred to one of the more isolated hotels for safekeeping. I phoned the hotel manager, who told me that the computers could not be operated there unless "a battalion of troops is sent to protect us against the mobs trying to stop the vote count." I called the president again. I told him that I was in the unprotected building and that there was no way to complete the election unless the workers could return with their computers. Also, I told him that our Secret Service would contact the White House if I didn't receive immediate protection from the mob outside.

Calm was restored after another hour, and the computers were tabulating returns by midnight. Our quick count showed that the ruling party would lose by about 14 percent, and early the next morning I went to visit both presidential candidates. They agreed to refrain from any public statements and to accept the final results, which were announced three days later. Cheddi Jagan was sworn in as president after what was considered to be the country's first free and fair election since independence. After his death five years later, his wife, Janet Jagan, became president, but she resigned in 1999 because of poor health.

The Carter Center has remained in close contact with the people of Guyana and has helped them to work out a long-range plan for economic and political development. A young deputy finance minister, Bharrat Jagdeo, was assigned by the Jagans to work with us on this project, and he performed this duty superbly. When Mrs. Jagan became ill, Jagdeo was chosen to succeed her as president, and he was elected and then reelected in 2001 and 2006. Unfortunately, many of the divisions in Guyana remain.

ZAMBIA ELECTION

Thousands of Zambians celebrate free elections in October 1991 with the singing of their national anthem. (ANTHONY ALLISON)

I have had many emotional experiences as the leader of The Carter Center, but one of my most unforgettable moments came in Lusaka, Zambia.

Since becoming president of Zambia in October 1964, Kenneth Kaunda had served as the undisputed leader of his nation for twenty-seven years. In 1991, however, he came under increasing pressure from his own people and from other African leaders to yield political power, and he decided to orchestrate a free national election. He had been a personal friend of mine while I was president, and he called me to invite a delegation from The Carter Center to monitor the process. In my conversations with Kenneth, it was obvious that, as the candidate of his UNIP political party, he expected to be endorsed overwhelmingly for an extended term.

This was our first experience as election observers in Africa, and we decided to invite a number of political leaders from the continent to join us. I was especially interested in having someone come from nearby South Africa to represent the African National Congress. Only a year earlier, the apartheid government had lifted the ban on the ANC as a political organization and released Nelson Mandela from prison. This was the first step toward a multiracial election that we hoped would be held in South Africa in the near future.

The Zambians were not accustomed to having a free choice in political affairs, and we worked very closely with the Electoral Commission and helped to train three thousand local election observers, with equal numbers to represent women, youth, labor, religion, education, and lawyers. Citizens were to vote in their home communities, and then all the ballot boxes were to be brought in to central locations, opened, and the results tabulated. As time for the election approached, fragmentary public opinion polls indicated that Frederick Chiluba, a labor leader from the copper mine area, would make a surprisingly strong showing. Although we had been invited by Kaunda, leaders of his UNIP party now began to condemn The Carter Center as "foreigners" who had come into Zambia to impose unwelcome Western restrictions on the voters.

Despite this intimidation, we decided to remain and dispersed our observer teams through all the regions of the country. On Election Day, I invited Dr. Franklin Sonn, the rector at Cape Technicon University, South Africa, and a leader of the ANC in South Africa, to accompany me. Our first polling site was a large open space among school buildings, and there were about ten tables where citizens were lined up to vote. As we entered the main door, Dr. Sonn burst into tears. I thought he must be ill, and asked if he needed to sit down or to have a drink of water. When he had partially regained his composure, he said, "I am fifty-three years old, and this is the first time I have ever seen anyone vote." We wept together for a few moments, and then we went about our duties.

Chiluba won that election, and three years later I noted with pleasure that President Nelson Mandela selected Dr. Sonn to be South Africa's ambassador to the United States.

The Carter Center and I have an intense interest in the People's Republic of China. President Richard Nixon had made a historic visit to China in 1972, and he and Chinese Premier Zhou Enlai signed the Shanghai Declaration, stating that there was "only one China" and that further steps should be taken to establish relations between our two nations. But no such progress was made because some of the more conservative Republican leaders in the United States continued to insist that the "one China" was Taiwan and that there should be no recognition of "Red China" on the mainland. It was not until six years later that I negotiated an agreement with the Chinese leader Deng Xiaoping to establish full diplomatic relations between the United States and the People's Republic and to sever such relations with Taiwan.

Deng Xiaoping accepted my invitation to visit the United States in January 1979, and we concluded a large number of agreements. During our private talks, the Chinese leader agreed to permit freedom of religion and the distribution of Bibles, and he expressed an interest in a more flexible policy toward individual economic freedom. Deng had a great sense of humor, and he was a hit with administration officials, the members of my family, and the news media and American public.

On one occasion I mentioned the Henry Jackson — Charles Vanik legislation that was designed to punish the Soviet Union for restricting the emigration of its Jewish citizens. Deng asked, "Do you mean that you want people from other nations to be free to move to America?"

"Yes, it is true that we object to people being deprived of their freedoms," I replied.

"Well, I'll be glad to send you five or ten million Chinese whenever you want them."

"Okay, and in return I'll send you twenty thousand of our extra lawyers."

After a moment, he replied, "You keep your lawyers; I'll keep my people."

After Deng returned to China, I sent my science adviser, Dr. Frank Press, to Beijing for follow-up discussions and was surprised to receive a telephone call from Frank one night, long after I had gone to bed.

He informed me that he was with Deng, who had asked him about sending Chinese students to study in American universities.

I responded, "Frank, I have already told you that we would welcome the students, and there would not be a limit."

He said, "Mr. President, he has asked me if they could send five thousand, and he wants an answer directly from you."

"Tell him to make it fifty thousand," I replied.

Although we were both surprised, the number of Chinese students passed this level within a few years, and before the end of the century there had been a total of 400,000 Chinese students enrolled in the American university system.

Although Deng Xiaoping invited me to make an immediate visit to China and to bring a small group of my family and close friends, I was preoccupied during the last months of my administration with the crisis of our embassy personnel being held captive in Iran and had to postpone accepting his invitation. However, one of my first foreign visits after leaving the White House was to China, in August 1981, accompanied by our invited group and by Michel Oksenberg, who was my Chinese adviser and fluent in their language. It was still a tightly controlled and regimented society, as illustrated by a confrontation our first day in Beijing.

Rosalynn and I had expressed a desire to take a bicycle ride from our guesthouse through a part of the city, and early the next morning we found bikes outside the front door — along with a great entourage of security personnel headed by an officious colonel.

He bowed slightly and informed me, "Sir, you may follow the first two vehicles in our motorcade."

I responded that I preferred to lead the way but that it would be acceptable for a few of them to follow at a discreet distance. We argued briefly, and he finally said that he had a map of Beijing and would outline a route that I could follow if I would wait a few minutes for a preliminary survey. Somewhat frustrated, I informed him that I would choose my own path and that their services would be welcomed if we encountered any kind of problem. After consulting with his subordinates, the colonel came to tell me that my request could not be honored.

Now quite annoyed, I ordered him to contact Deng Xiaoping personally and ascertain whether I would be free, as his personal guest, to choose my own route or whether I was to be regimented by a colonel in his security force. I would wait in the guesthouse. I went inside and slammed the door, and within a few minutes there was a timid knock. I was informed that I was free to travel wherever I wished and there was no reason to appeal to higher authorities. Throughout our remaining ten days of traveling in the country, we jogged or rode bikes each morning with no interference. We could stop along the way to buy some tea or freshly baked bread, join in or observe the tai chi exercises, accept an invitation to visit with a family in their home, or just move with the traffic flow. At that time, there were few automobiles in Beijing, but hundreds of bicycles responded to directions at each major intersection.

We soon learned that for weeks before our arrival Chinese television had repeated over and over the news broadcasts of our normalization ceremonies and the visits of Deng and his wife with our family in Washington. We were the center of attention wherever we went, and sometimes as we wandered down a main street, pausing to look at a window display or make a small purchase, we would glance back to see several hundred Chinese following at a respectful distance and applauding when we acknowledged their presence.

My official talks with the vice premier were interrupted frequently with peals of laughter as we recalled his earlier experiences in Texas, Georgia, and with us in Washington. He was very eager for me to visit the rural areas of China, where he had just initiated the first phase of economic freedom. He made it plain that this process would be expedited but that he would not permit any structural change in the Communist Party system. He outlined, however, a plan that would permit small rural villages to begin having elections, since larger cities, counties, and provinces chose Communist delegates to participate in making political decisions on the national level.

We went into the countryside whenever possible and witnessed the first careful steps toward what was to be a startling and revolutionary free-enterprise system in China. For the first time, farm families were permitted to cultivate up to 15 percent of land for themselves after fulfilling their duties within the government's cooperatives. They could sell their products and retain the profits for their own use. Although their personal land was usually around the edges of fields, in the shade, or in ditches, production was very high — because it was theirs. Families on farms or in some very small designated rural villages could also have one project for personal profit: grow up to five pigs, chickens, or ducks; repair bicycles; shoe horses; make nails; or mold clay pots. Deng told me later he realized that a sick cooperative hog might die, but that a family would stay up all night to nurse their own hog back to health. He intended to expand economic freedom one step at a time.

Before leaving China, I asked Deng if it would be permissible for The Carter Center to originate some kind of project that might be beneficial to his people. At first he declined, but then he promised to consider my offer. I knew that his son Deng Pufang had been pushed from a third-story window during the Cultural Revolution and was a paraplegic, and Deng Xiaoping agreed when I asked if we could consult his son for some ideas. Within a few months after returning home, we launched two successful programs. One was to teach nine hundred Chinese teachers how to educate deaf or blind students, and the other was to help design and construct a large facility to manufacture prostheses of the most advanced design. Rosalynn and I later returned to China to commemorate the completion of these projects.

Since it began in 1996, our most ambitious and sustained program in China has been to monitor and encourage the evolution of democratic elections in about 650,000 small villages that are not included in the Communist Party structure of government. Started under the direction of Robert Pastor, this China Village Elections Project affects about 75 percent of the nation's 1.3 billion people. A basic law (similar to our Constitution) was adopted in 1982 authorizing the holding of such political contests, and in 1987 the process was made mandatory. The Carter Center was later asked by the Chinese government to monitor and encourage compliance of villages with the law, and to help them develop and distribute a computer database to describe the status of this project. At first, top Chinese officials discouraged any publicity about the program, but later they revealed what is being done.

With the project now headed by Yawei Liu, our Center provides suggestions for the improvement of the Chinese laws and has been invited to observe direct elections of National People's Congress deputies at the township and county levels. We have also invited representatives of the NPC to observe elections in the United States and have had officials assigned to work at The Carter Center. In 2005, the name of our project was changed to the China Program, and we established the website www.chinaelections.org, available in both Chinese and English, which lets scholars worldwide study Chinese politics and offer suggestions for reform. Our program also maintains the Chinese-language website www.chinarural.org, which permits national and global exchanges on grassroots democracy. The China Program has been an initiative of Chinese officials, and this involvement of our Center has been very gratifying.

Observing villagers electing five members of their local governing bodies has been especially interesting. All citizens of a village are automatically registered to vote when they reach the age of eighteen, and there is considerable peer pressure to participate on Election Day. There is no requirement that voters or candidates be members of the Communist Party. The villagers assemble in the town square, usually seated on small portable stools, and listen carefully as the qualified candidates make brief campaign speeches. Then voters go forward to mark their paper ballots, carefully guarding the secrecy of their choices. When all voters have returned to their seats, the ballots are emptied onto a tabletop and counted aloud, while tabulators indicate the running totals on a prominent blackboard.

With the final results known, the successful candidates are inducted into their offices — the equivalents of American mayors and city councils. Their terms are three years, and they can seek reelection. Often when they do run again, their previous tape-recorded campaign speeches are replayed,

In Shidong village in China, election staff bring a roving ballot box to the house of a disabled citizen, Mr. Xu Rongkui, age seventy, who cannot travel to the polling station to vote. (JIAN YI)

so there is a high turnover among office-holders who don't fulfill their promises. Most of the campaign speeches I have heard consisted of entrepreneurial promises relating to economic projects for the villagers, such as planting a number of pear trees, producing starch from locally grown corn, or processing high-quality meat from swine or poultry. One memorable speech was about the replacement of public toilets that had been removed by the provincial government to build a highway.

Top officials have made it clear that this democratic process at the village level does not assume that it will supplant the cherished system of the Communist Party, in which leaders of each successively higher level are chosen in a caucus procedure. Some communities have also developed a conflict between the authority of elected village officials and the authority of Party officials who are reluctant to relinquish their control over local affairs. So far, the NPC has not resolved this question.

PALESTINE

One of our most sustained commitments has been to help bring peace to Israel and its neighbors, but this has been a tortuous and frustrating process. Pope John Paul II once declared that two solutions were possible to the Palestinian-Israeli conflict: the realistic and the miraculous. The realistic would involve a divine intervention, from heaven; the miraculous would be a voluntary agreement between the two parties!

It may be difficult for readers to remember what I faced as a new president concerning the nation of Israel. There was an oil embargo by Arab OPEC nations, with a secondary boycott against any American corporation doing business with Israel. There had been four major wars in twenty-five years led by Egypt, the only Arab country (then with Soviet military support) that had the status of a formidable challenger. The United States had not made any concerted efforts to bring a comprehensive peace to Israel, America's closest ally in the Middle East, and there were no demands on me to initiate such negotiations. There had never been a national site in America to commemorate the Nazi Holocaust. And the Soviet Union was permitting only a handful of Jews to emigrate each year.

As president, I began to communicate publicly with noted human rights heroes in the Soviet Union like Andrei Sakharov and Natan Sharansky, and to confront Soviet leaders publicly on their behalf. This contact increased tensions between me and Soviet President Leonid Brezhnev, but within two years annual Jewish immigration to the United States from Russia increased to more than fifty thousand.

We also supported legislation that prohibited secondary boycotts against Israel, with the imposition of severe penalties against any U.S. corporation that violated the new law. In 1978, on Israel's thirtieth birthday, with Israeli Prime Minister Menachem Begin and several hundred rabbis present on the South Lawn of the White House, I announced that a blue-ribbon commission would establish a Holocaust memorial. With the noted Holocaust survivor Elie Wiesel as its chairman, the commission's work resulted in the Holocaust Museum in Washington.

As one of my highest priorities, I negotiated the Camp David Accords between Israel and Egypt in 1978; in them, in exchange for peace, security, and good neighborly relations, Israel agreed to grant full autonomy to the Palestinians and to withdraw Israeli military and political forces from the Egyptian Sinai, the West Bank, and Gaza. This agreement was ratified by an 85 percent majority in the Israeli parliament. Six months later we concluded a peace treaty between Israel and Egypt, not a word of which has

Mrs. Carter records their observations as she and the former U.S. president witness voting in a polling station in the West Bank during the January 2006 Palestinian Legislative Council elections. (DEBORAH HAKES)

been violated for more than twenty-eight years. This agreement removed from Israel its major Arab military threat.

I left office believing that Israel would soon realize the dream of peace with its other neighbors, becoming a small nation no longer beleaguered. It would exemplify the finest ideals based on the Hebrew Scriptures that I have taught on Sundays since I was eighteen years old, where, in the English-language version, "justice" is mentioned 28 times and "righteousness" 196 times.

Representing The Carter Center, Rosalynn and I traveled regularly throughout the Middle East in an effort to explore every opportunity to encourage peaceful relations between Israel and its Arab neighbors. There were times when President Reagan's national security advisers asked me to discuss confidential matters with heads of state. The Center's Middle East fellow Kenneth Stein was helpful with his knowledge of Israel's history, and he and my assistant Faye Perdue attended most of the sessions that were not confidential or did not involve official matters. We were able to travel extensively in the West Bank and Gaza.

Although I had met earlier with other PLO leaders in Egypt and Syria, my first personal meeting with Yasir Arafat was during a visit to Paris in April 1990. He knew that I had called for a Palestinian homeland and pointed out that a democratic process would have to be the first step, and he urged me to consider helping to ensure that someday Palestinians could elect their own government. I promised that, when the time came for any kind of election, The Carter Center and I would be committed — provided we could obtain approval from Israel. One provision of the 1993 Oslo Agreement was that Palestinians could establish their own governing authority and elect their leaders, and this was scheduled for January 1996.

After obtaining approval from Israel and the White House, we prepared a highly qualified observer team, some members of which arrived well in advance of the election to become thoroughly familiar with the laws and regulations that would govern the process, the candidates for office, and the sensitive relationship between Israeli officials and the Palestinians.

It was obvious that the Israelis had almost complete control over every aspect of the political, military, and economic existence of Palestinians within the West Bank and Gaza. Israeli settlements permeated the Occupied Territories, and highways connecting the settlements with one another and with

Jerusalem were being rapidly built, with Palestinians prohibited from using or crossing some of the key roads. In addition, almost five hundred Israeli checkpoints obstructed the routes still open to Palestinian pedestrian and vehicular traffic.

I learned on arrival that the blue-ribbon Elections Commission had been in existence for only four weeks and that political candidates had just three weeks to campaign, but that seven hundred had qualified for the eighty-eight legislative council seats, six of which were set aside for Christians and one for a Samaritan. Only Arafat and a relatively unknown woman named Samiha Khalil had qualified for the presidency.

There seemed to be many unnecessary restraints imposed by the Israelis, and I discussed them with Prime Minister Shimon Peres and General Uri Dayan, who was responsible for security in the West Bank and Gaza. They assured me that key checkpoints would be opened, Israeli soldiers would not enter voting places, and voters would not be intimidated. The biggest problem related to East Jerusalem, which Palestinians (and the international community) consider occupied territory and Israel claims as an integral part of its nation.

There were about 120,000 registered Arab

voters in East Jerusalem, only about 4,000 of whom would be given Israeli permits to vote — and then only in five post offices, four of them quite small. At Arafat's request, I met with leaders of Hamas, an Islamic militant group that opposed recognition of Israel, perpetrated acts of violence, and was increasingly competitive with Arafat's secular Fatah Party. I urged them to accept the results of the election and forgo violence. They promised not to disrupt the elections and to renounce violence in the future "if Israelis discontinue repression." They informed me that they intended to participate in later municipal elections but not to be part of the Palestinian parliament.

At the last minute we ran into a serious problem over the ballot boxes in East Jerusalem. The Israelis insisted that the slots be on the side, as in a post office. The Palestinians wanted the slots on top so they could drop their ballots in. We finally worked out a compromise: to have the slots on the top corners! Palestinians could claim they were dropping in their ballots vertically while Israelis could maintain that they were being inserted horizontally.

The procedures during the election were practically perfect. There was a huge turnout in the West Bank and Gaza. Arafat was elected overwhelmingly, and Fatah parliamentary candidates prevailed, but some strong independents were also elected, including Hanan Ashrawi, an influential Christian spokesperson from Ramallah. Everyone laughed when Arafat told me there were going to be about fifteen women on the council, adding, "Hanan counts for ten."

Prime Minister Peres announced that all members of the Palestinian Legislative Council would be permitted to travel freely within the West Bank and Gaza to participate in the parliament. All of us international observers were pleased with the quality of the election, which we considered an overwhelming mandate for formation of a Palestinian government and for reconciliation between Israelis and Palestinians. We were of course mindful of the extreme sensitivity and difficulty of issues still to be resolved.

Yasir Arafat died in November 2004, and Palestinian law required that his successor be elected within a few weeks. Once again, The Carter Center was asked to observe the process. I arrived in Israel on January 6, 2005. My first meeting was with Prime Minister Ariel Sharon, who told me that Israeli checkpoints would be manned by soldiers during the Palestinian election but that they would not impede traffic, and that military forces would be withdrawn from the major cities. Having observed Sharon in action for almost three decades, I had no doubt that he would fulfill his promises. I urged him to be flexible in permitting Palestinians to vote in East Jerusalem. He replied that the arrangements of 1996 would prevail, reminding me that I had been instrumental in negotiating the agreements. He added that no Palestinian polling officials or domestic observers would be allowed to enter the post offices, which would be manned only by Israeli employees.

Our practice as observers is that we move constantly throughout Election Day, visiting as many voting sites as possible. I began my day with the post offices in East Jerusalem, where problems always seemed to have arisen. It soon became apparent that the Israeli officials had voters' lists that were different from the names of people who came to cast ballots, and by noon there had been practically no voting — just a growing crowd of angry Palestinians. At the main polling site, the only post office larger than a mobile home, there were 3,500 names on the list. One Israeli clerk was checking the credentials of potential voters and methodically turning them away.

When I finally threatened to call an international press conference, the prime minister's office agreed to ignore the lists and permit all persons registered in Jerusalem to vote at any site, but with only international observers and no Palestinians monitoring the process. It was now 2:00 P.M., and we were able to salvage the participation of only a small number of voters. Our observers reported no significant problems in the West Bank or Gaza.

Early the next morning, Carter Center leaders assessed the reports of our observer teams. I prepared a private letter of advice for delivery to Mahmoud Abbas, who had been elected president overwhelmingly. He was a strong and moderate leader who had always espoused good-faith peace talks with Israel. The Israelis, having ruled out any negotiation with Arafat, now would have the negotiating partner they had seemed to want.

It was on this trip that we would see the most disturbing intrusions of the great dividing wall Israel was building. Described as a "security fence" whose declared function was to deter Palestinian attacks against Israelis, its other purpose became clear as we observed its construction and examined maps of the barrier's ultimate path through

Palestine. Including the Israeli-occupied Jordan River Valley, the wall would take in large areas of land for Israel and completely encircle Palestinians who remained in their remnant of the West Bank, as was already the case with Gaza. This configuration would severely restrict Palestinian access to the outside world and make any peace agreement almost impossible.

After returning to America, I went to the White House and gave a personal report to President George W. Bush. I emphasized my concern about the building of the wall and relayed Mahmoud Abbas's desire to begin comprehensive peace talks at an early date. The president repeated his commitment to the peace process and said that his new secretary of state, Condoleezza Rice, was taking office that same day and one of her top priorities would be a persistent and aggressive search for a "two-state solution" between Israel and the Palestinians. Unfortunately, the war in Iraq and other issues have prevented this effort.

Although all Palestinian elections were models of organization, honesty, and peacefulness, the third one, in January 2006, was extremely controversial. On the one hand, Hamas candidates had done well in municipal elections throughout the Occupied Territories, had governed well, had a cohesive political organization, and had for sixteen months observed a unilateral cease-fire that they called a *hudna*. On the other hand, Fatah had been in existence for many years and was riddled with internal competitions, and some of their leaders had been accused of corruption. Opinion polls showed that Hamas would win about 35 percent of the votes. Neither Fatah nor Israel wanted to proceed with the election, but the United States insisted it occur, so it was scheduled almost exactly ten years after the Palestinian National Authority was formed.

This time there were several international observer groups to witness the election of 132 members of the Palestinian Legislative Council. With Ariel Sharon incapacitated by illness, Rosalynn and I met with acting Prime Minister Ehud Olmert, whom we had known for more than twenty years. Carter Center leaders also met with other Israeli and Palestinian leaders — with one exception. To obtain approval from Washington for our participation, we had to promise not to talk to any Hamas candidates or political leaders before the election.

Hamas won a surprising victory, with 42 percent of the popular vote. They had taken full advantage of the election laws and had qualified only one candidate for each position, whereas Fatah sometimes had several. Hamas won seventy-four contests, giving them a clear majority of parliamentary seats. Our conflict resolution director, Matthew Hodes, and I urged Mahmoud Abbas to join in a unity government, but he refused. All of Fatah's cabinet members resigned. Subsequently, the United States and Israel orchestrated an economic boycott against the Palestinian people. Abbas remained president of the Palestinian National Authority and also head of the PLO, which is the only Palestinian organization recognized by Israel, the United Nations, or the United States.

A unity government was finally formed, and then disrupted by conflict between Hamas and Fatah in Gaza. Still, after almost seven years, no peace talks between Israel and the Palestinians have been conducted. The Carter Center will stay engaged in the Middle East with a full-time office in the West Bank. I decided to describe the plight of the Palestinian people and invite a debate on the lack of a peace effort by writing the book *Palestine Peace Not Apartheid.*

Few from outside the Middle East have had a greater opportunity than we at The Carter Center to understand the complex political and personal interrelationships in the region. We are familiar with the harsh rhetoric and extreme acts of violence against innocent civilians, and we understand the fear among many Israelis of threats against their safety and even their existence as a nation. During all these years, we have reiterated our strong condemnation of any acts of violence against civilians, which are not justified at any time or for any goal.

Our continuing effort will be to bring peace, with justice, to Israel and its neighbors, and our nongovernmental character gives us a singular opportunity to pursue all avenues to achieve this objective. Some of our most valuable allies are B'Tselem and Al-Haq, two effective human rights organizations that represent the viewpoints of Israelis and Palestinians, respectively.

VENEZUELA

Under the leadership of Dr. Jennifer McCoy, The Carter Center has been deeply involved in Venezuela's election processes for almost a decade. Late in 1998 we were invited by all political factions to monitor the presidential elections, with public opinion polls indicating that a supposedly radical candidate, Lieutenant Colonel Hugo Chávez, would be the likely victor. He had been imprisoned as the leader of an attempted coup in 1992, and was later pardoned by President Rafael Caldera Rodríguez. Chávez now advocated a public referendum to form a "constituent assembly" that would write a new constitution. Senior military officers were fearful of him, while most junior officers and enlisted men were supportive. Among private citizens, there was an overwhelming desire to see drastic but peaceful political changes, and the formerly dominant political parties were in disrepute, with only one of them nominating a candidate.

Designed to bring some order out of chaos and to eliminate fraud, a $150 million optical-scan voting system, produced in the United States, had been acquired and installed in seven thousand polling places by Spanish experts, to record each ballot, tabulate the count, and transmit the final results instantaneously to central locations.

All observers accepted the fact that Venezuela had been terribly mismanaged and shot through with corruption, and was something of an economic basket case, with a deficit equal to 8 percent of its national budget, crude oil prices less than eight dollars a barrel, and extremely high unemployment and inflation. Despite these intransigent problems, campaign rhetoric had raised excessive expectations among the poor and working class. The former Bolivian president Gonzalo Sánchez de Lozada and I visited Caracas together and had a forceful exchange with Chávez about his proposal to establish a constituent assembly that would not only write a new constitution but would also abolish the existing congress, or remove some of its important legislative functions. We emphasized that the international community would most likely question this move unless the elected congress could continue to serve until a new constitution could be approved. Chávez listened carefully but seemed reluctant to change his position.

One week before the election, the old political parties shifted all their support to the other leading candidate, Henrique Salas Romer, in an attempt to prevent a Chávez victory. We had a strong monitoring team of forty members from nine nations, managed by Jennifer McCoy. The former Chilean president Patricio Aylwin Azócar joined Gonzalo Sánchez de Lozada and shared the leadership of our Carter Center delegation with me and former U.S. Treasury Secretary Nicholas Brady. Polls predicted that Chávez would win a clear victory, and he ultimately gained 57 percent of the vote.

Subsequently, we observed the referendum that approved a new constitution, and in

May 2000 we flew to Venezuela to monitor the resulting election but learned during the flight that the Supreme Court had postponed it because of obvious lack of preparation. There were more than 33,000 candidates for 6,000 positions, with 1,300 different ballots, combined with the world's most advanced electronic vote tabulation system. The election was held two months later. General Francisco Arias Cárdenas publicly claimed victory early in the evening, based on his own exit poll results, but our quick count and returns from the electoral commission showed that Chávez was being reelected by a wide margin, with his coalition winning about 60 percent of the parliamentary seats and more than half of the governorships. Overall, the election was peaceful, and the results seemed to represent the will of the people, at least in the presidential contest.

In April 2002, a temporary coup removed President Chávez from office for two days, but condemnations from Latin American leaders and public demonstrations in Venezuela resulted in his being returned to power. There was a general belief that the United States gave at least tacit support for the coup attempt, and harsh statements by President Chávez about the Bush administration increasingly strained relations between our two countries.

Following the coup, President Chávez requested that I facilitate a dialogue between the major political groups, and in July 2002 Jennifer McCoy and I went to Caracas to explore this possibility. The major opposition forces had consolidated within an organization called Coordinadora Democrática, and, along with the OAS, we were invited to a somewhat fiery meeting at their headquarters. Their final decision was that none of the opposition groups would participate in any dialogue with government officials at that time and that they would find "other means" to resolve controversial issues at a later date. Obviously in the driver's seat, Chávez was personable, friendly, and taking full advantage of his popularity among the poor, with the new constitution having concentrated power in the executive that let him control almost all public institutions. We formed a partnership with the OAS and UNDP, and initiated a sustained effort to mediate between the opposing political groups. Multiple street confrontations and a two-month petroleum strike began in December 2002 and disrupted the normal economic, financial, and political processes of the nation.

Early in 2003, after fishing for peacock

bass in southern Venezuela, I returned to Caracas and met with President Chávez and his adversaries. I spelled out two options for resolving the conflict: one was a constitutional amendment providing for early elections and the other compliance with provisions of the constitution dealing with a recall of elected public officials. In May of that year, we helped to negotiate a pact based on the second option, which would permit the opposition to seek signatures of 20 percent of the 12,180,000 registered voters. This would automatically trigger a recall referendum on whether Chávez could complete his six-year term.

A five-member election commission (CNE) was created by the Supreme Court to supervise all elections and referenda. Although the commission was ostensibly balanced, it was generally known that the chairman and two members were pro-government. Following the collection of 3,477,000 signatures, the National Election Commission accepted 1,911,000 of them as legitimate, rejected 375,000 as invalid, and declared the authenticity of approximately 1.2 million names doubtful. This meant that 525,000 of the doubtful ones would have to be reaffirmed to meet the 20 percent requirement. After five months of controversy, both sides finally agreed with our proposal that a three-day period would be devoted to having these names reconfirmed by the individual voters, and the electoral commission decided that previous confirmed signers could withdraw their names. Chávez assured us he was completely reconciled to participating in the recall referendum if the 20 percent requirement was reached.

Careful assessment of the signatures revealed that a recall referendum was approved, and in August The Carter Center and the Organization of American States deployed approximately 160 observers throughout the nation, with Jennifer McCoy as head of our delegation. Because of the importance of this referendum, I decided to expand the leadership of the delegation to include the former presidents Raúl Alfonsin (Argentina), Belisario Betancur (Colombia), Rodrigo Carazo (Costa Rica), and Eduardo Duhalde (Argentina). Our group met with President Chávez, who pledged to resign immediately if he should lose the referendum vote and said in that case he would rest for a week and then resume campaigning for reelection. Our next meeting was with opposition leaders, who presented a litany of catastrophic predictions about cheating, intimidation, and actual violence planned by the government for Election Day. The Latin American leaders were able to answer most of their concerns.

At about noon, the opposition leaders presented to us and their supporters what turned out to be false exit polling data that showed Chávez losing the vote by twenty points or more, and they distributed this information widely to their own people and to foreign news media. Shortly after midnight, our group and the OAS secretary-general, César Gaviria, visited election headquarters to witness the first electronic tabulation, which showed Chávez prevailing with 57 percent of the votes out of the 6.6 million counted at that time. Gaviria and I decided to invite the private news media owners and other opposition leaders to my hotel suite to share these results and to tell them that they were compatible with our own quick count results. Some of those present said they would accept the official tally, while others were angry or resentful, claiming the entire vote was fraudulent. Final results showed 58 to 42 percent in favor of Chávez, with him prevailing in twenty-two of the twenty-four states.

Some opposition leaders were still in anguish, as indicated by morning newspaper editorial headlines: "Catástrofe," "El Fraude Permanente," and "Serias Dudas." Their crusade was expanded to the United States, where they convinced *The Wall Street Journal* and some Washington officials to join in their claim of massive election fraud. Our subsequent analyses showed a close correlation between the electronic returns and the paper ballot receipts that were required for substantiation of the results.

Involvement of The Carter Center in the political affairs of Venezuela has been limited since this referendum. Subsequent election returns have shown a solid majority of popular votes for Hugo Chávez, who has used this advantage to consolidate increasing power in his office, to capture total control over the legislature, and to orchestrate membership in the judiciary. During this time, high prices for oil have provided the government with enormous income, which can be spent in ways that retain or increase political support for the ruling power. We monitor the situation closely and remain prepared to lend our services in the future to improve democratic electoral policies and relationships both among factions within the country and between Venezuela and the United States.

INDONESIA

Perhaps the most significant election that has been monitored by The Carter Center was in Indonesia, and our opportunity was just an accident. In 1997, Georgia state officials asked if I would meet a man who had designed a midsize airplane that could be quickly changed from a configuration for hauling passengers to one for carrying cargo. He was from Indonesia. He wanted to build a manufacturing plant in the Southeast, preferably Georgia or Alabama. We soon welcomed Bacharuddin Jusuf Habibie to our home in Plains. He asked us to call him B.J., told us that he was minister in charge of science and technology under President Suharto, had a doctorate in aeronautical engineering from Germany, and was eager to produce and sell his airplane in Western nations. He was exuberant, smiled a lot, and answered all my questions. Rosalynn served us sandwiches for lunch as I extolled the advantages of building his factory in Georgia. He was attentive but seemed to be more eager to learn about the work of The Carter Center. We exchanged telephone numbers before he left.

We were amazed a few months later to read that our friend B.J. had become vice president of Indonesia, and I called to congratulate him. President Suharto was forced to resign in May 1998, and Habibie became president of the fourth-largest nation on earth. Rosalynn and I learned that Indonesia's 235 million inhabitants were divided into one hundred ethnic groups and spoke three hundred different languages and dialects. Of the total population, 87 percent were Muslims, making Indonesia by far the largest Islamic nation. The secular and authoritarian government had been led by two former generals, Sukarno and Suharto, since becoming independent at the end of World War II in 1945.

Instead of clinging to office, B. J. Habibie resolved to have an honest and fair election, and he called to ask me if The Carter Center would be willing to help with the arrangements and monitor the process. An exploratory visit by our staff in March 1999 revealed that officials of the government, the national election commission (KPU), major political parties, the military, and domestic monitoring groups all desired our participation. I notified the president that we would accept his invitation.

This would be the largest and most complex democratic procedure in which we had ever participated. We formed a partnership with the National Democratic Institute. The KPU shaped a step-by-step process: first to elect 462 members of parliament by popular vote, to which would be added 38 from the

Supporters rally for one of five presidential candidates in Indonesia's 2004 election. (JOSHUA ESTEY)

military, 5 each to represent the twenty-seven provinces, and 65 more chosen by the KPU from "unrepresented groups." These 700 would constitute the People's National Assembly, with full authority to make laws and to elect the next president. This process was scheduled to be completed early in November.

Forty-eight political parties qualified for the June election that we would monitor, to present a total of 13,800 candidates for local, provincial, and national office, at about 300,000 polling sites. The key issue was whether the various "reform" parties would prevail over Golkar, the party of Suharto and Habibie. Another question in Indonesia was whether the more deeply religious Muslims would move the government toward Islamic law. Although nearly 90 percent of the population was Muslim, public opinion polls showed that there was a strong preference for a secular government.

A number of international organizations, including the Asia Society, had joined us and the National Democratic Institute in training almost 300,000 domestic observers and establishing a reporting system for election returns and a quick count procedure based on returns from nine thousand statistically representative polling sites.

Rosalynn and I flew to Indonesia a few days early with one of our Center's trustees, Richard Blum, on his private plane, and we took our youngest son, Jeffrey. Jeff had concentrated his studies on Indonesia and knew the names of all the cabinet members, top military officers, political candidates, religious leaders, and others who shaped the nation's policies and character. We decided to take a close look at one of the provinces and, not surprisingly, chose Bali, where we stayed in a small hotel in the interior of the island. Our first impression was of the large posters and thousands of red flags along the roads, not more than twenty yards apart for miles, representing the PDI-P party of Megawati Sukarnoputri, the daughter of the former president Sukarno, whose mother was Balinese. More remarkable was that at daybreak two days later, every campaign advertisement in Bali had disappeared, as required by law!

Bali lived up to all expectations — as a truly lovely place, with gentle and beautiful people, whose Hindu culture was the dominant force in everyday life in the area we visited. We took long treks through the countryside and observed that each home was, in effect, a Hindu temple, with votive offerings of fruit and flowers prepared daily for display in houses, rice fields, and other places, and effigies of the good and evil gods almost always in sight.

After a few days we flew to Yogyakarta to visit the huge and ornate Buddhist temple at Borobudur, then joined our monitoring delegation in Jakarta. We had a total of one hundred observers from twenty-three nations, who were thoroughly briefed and then dispatched to different provinces.* We had an extensive press conference and met with President Habibie and his cabinet, domestic observers, leaders of major parties, and the national election commission.

On voting day, Rosalynn and I went to our assigned sites in Jakarta and around the periphery of the city. The procedures were followed meticulously, the turnout was about 90 percent, and everyone seemed to be in good spirits. All the polling sites had been erected just for this purpose, outdoors but sheltered from the sun and rain, ranging from hand-made bamboo frames covered with plastic to elaborate fringed canopies decorated with colorful cloth bows and orchids. Since the KPU allotted only five thousand rupiah

---

* Not including East Timor, which the international community did not recognize as part of Indonesia, since it was taken by force from Portugal.

(about sixty-five cents) to each community, the citizens had to use their own contributions and initiative for the shelters.

At the close of the voting, at 2:00 P.M., each ballot was examined and the vote was called out for everyone to hear. There was a festive atmosphere, with cheers or boos from the crowd after each vote was announced. This was the first time in more than fifty years that the citizens had been free to make their own choices.

Although it would be several weeks before final and official results were known, the first reports from our nine thousand representative sites indicated that Mrs. Megawati's party would receive 36 percent, Habibie's Golkar Party 23 percent, and three religious parties about 10 percent each. The choice of president by a majority vote of the seven hundred parliamentarians would be unrestricted, possibly a respected business, religious, or academic leader who had not been a candidate.

Before leaving Jakarta, I received Habibie's permission to meet with Xanana Gusmão, the imprisoned leader from East Timor. He had been held incommunicado, but when I later visited the president, he agreed to permit Gusmão to meet with the two East Timorese Catholic bishops, some expatriates,

A polling official announces each vote, one by one, to assembled citizens, then shows them the marked ballot, as votes are tallied in a Jakarta polling station during Indonesia's 2004 elections. (Joshua Estey)

and a half dozen others from the province to decide how best to prepare for a referendum to determine whether East Timor would be independent or remain a part of Indonesia. Habibie also approved the participation of The Carter Center, the United Nations, and perhaps other international observers to help ensure a safe and free decision on this question. We participated for several months in East Timor's successful move to independence.

We returned home uncertain about the presidential election process but convinced that the Indonesians had made a commitment to freedom and democracy, and would soon become the third-largest democracy in the world.

In November 1999, the parliament chose a respected religious leader, Abdurrahman Wahid (Gus Dur), as president and Megawati Sukarnoputri as vice president. Wahid's policies aroused intense opposition, and in July 2001 he ordered Susilo Bambang Yudhoyono (known as SBY), minister for politics and security, to declare a state of emergency. Yudhoyono refused, and Wahid removed him from his position. The parliament voted to impeach Wahid and replace him with Megawati. During her term in office, the election laws were changed to permit a direct vote for president.

Once again, in 2004, Rosalynn and I headed The Carter Center monitoring team under the direction of David Carroll (Democracy Program director), and Yudhoyono defeated President Megawati and other candidates in another honest, fair, and peaceful process. We congratulated him and paid our respects to Mrs. Megawati on July 7, which happened to be our fifty-eighth wedding anniversary.

On the way home we stopped to spend six days fishing for rainbow trout in the pristine Zhupanova River in the Kamchatka Peninsula of Russia. (It was interesting to note that we were closer to New York than to Moscow.)

In Washington and in the U.S. news media there is an obsession with violence and terrorism, and a pervasive derogation of Muslims. The people of Indonesia are providing a dramatic example of peaceful political change and firmly negating the claim that Muslim societies are averse to democratic governments. Of the world's three largest democracies, the overwhelming majority of their populations have different religious faiths: Hindus in India, Christians in the United States, and Muslims in Indonesia. This is a good message for the world to absorb.

Nigeria is the most populous and perhaps the most influential nation in Africa, but also the most disappointing in adopting democracy and controlling government corruption.

Olusegun Obasanjo was a contemporary of mine as president, having become the leader of Nigeria as a general and then deciding to relinquish political authority to a popularly elected successor. It was because of my friendship with Obasanjo that I decided to visit his country and Liberia in 1978, the first trip by a U.S. president to sub-Saharan Africa. After he and I left office, we worked together to help resolve some of the challenges faced by other African nations. Later, under the regime of a despotic military dictator, Sani Abacha, Obasanjo was imprisoned because of his public condemnation of the regime's corruption and human rights abuses. I went to see Abacha and convinced him to permit Obasanjo to return to his farm home, where he was kept under house arrest. He was subsequently detained again and remained under arrest until after the death of Abacha, in June 1998.

We at The Carter Center were pleased to be asked to participate as observers of Nigeria's national elections in 1999, the first to be held in the country in sixteen years. I was also glad when Obasanjo decided to seek the presidency, but I was determined to remain neutral between him and the other candidate, Olu Falae, a graduate of Yale University and former finance minister. I visited Nigeria in January to meet with the Independent National Electoral Commission, acting head of state General Abdulsalami Abubakar, the two prominent candidates, chairmen of the political parties, and other leaders. We considered this one of the most important elections to be held that year, because of the size and influence of Nigeria on the African continent and because of the need to end the history of military rule, imposed during twenty-eight of the thirty-eight years of national independence.

The Center formed an alliance with the National Democratic Institute and invited the former Niger president Mahamane Ousmane and U.S. General Colin Powell, former chairman of the Joint Chiefs of Staff (and future secretary of state), to be my co-chairs. There were sixty-six people from ten nations in our delegation, and our teams were sent to their assigned locations in states where problems had been detected and their presence would be most beneficial.

The day before the election, Rosalynn,

the Center's democracy program director Charles Costello, and I flew to Port Harcourt for meetings with representatives of the Niger Delta community. We knew that the region was a tinderbox. Although we found all representatives, including those of the militant Ijaw youth, to be searching for a peaceful resolution of their grievances against the oil companies and the government, no one expressed confidence in the current series of elections or the ability of elected local or state officials to address their needs. These intelligent young leaders quietly declared that their more influential elders had not been permitted to register and that, in any case, it was fruitless to vote because election officials were bribed to report results without regard to how ballots were cast. I urged them to give the process a chance to succeed and to work with the elected officials who would be taking office on May 29.

Unfortunately, on Election Day we found that the predictions of the Ijaw young people were accurate in many states. Rosalynn and I observed election reports of high turnout when very few people actually voted and many instances of ballot-box stuffing, with stacks of ballots removed from the boxes in sequential order and all marked with the same fingerprint. Few people seemed to have been voting in Bayelsa State, for instance, where there were 497,333 people registered. The reported returns were that a total of 610,032 ballots were counted, overwhelmingly for General Obasanjo. All of our observers saw instances of false and inflated tally sheets being substituted for the original ones, along with many technical errors, such as failure to use indelible ink, late arrival of ballots, and absence of voting secrecy.

My assessment was that state governors, many of them former army generals, had decided that their fellow officer Obasanjo should be elected and had taken actions to ensure his victory. The final claim was that he received 62.6 percent of the votes. I issued the following statement on behalf of The Carter Center:

> There was a wide disparity between the number of voters observed at the polling stations and the final results that have been reported from several states. Regrettably, therefore, it is not possible for us to make an accurate judgment about the outcome of the presidential election.

We met with the defeated candidate Olu Falae and urged him to reject violence and present his proof of fraud to the electoral commission and the federal courts. He did so, and his claims were rejected. There were serious demonstrations, with at least fourteen people killed in protest over the conduct of the election.

We retained our presence in Nigeria to continue a wide range of projects, including agricultural improvement and efforts to eradicate Guinea worm and to deal with schistosomiasis, lymphatic filariasis, onchocerciasis, and trachoma. We presumed that the election processes would be dramatically improved before the next national contests, in 2003. As that time approached, however, it became obvious that few reforms had been introduced, and we refused an invitation to participate as observers. Obasanjo captured 61.8 percent of the votes in another fraudulent election, condemned by the European Union, the National Democratic Institute, and other international monitoring teams. In the sharply divided and disgruntled Niger Delta area, his party won almost 100 percent of the reported votes.

As the time for elections approached once more, in 2007, President Obasanjo sought to have the constitution amended to permit him a third term, but a surprisingly independent National Assembly refused to ratify the change. Umaru Yar'Adua, a relatively unknown Muslim governor of a remote northern state, was elected as his successor. Tragically for the Nigerian people and as a terrible example for other countries on the troubled continent, this third fraudulent election was also condemned by both local and international observers.

There are some encouraging signs in this great nation. After the longest period of civilian rule in the country's history, it is unlikely that the citizens would accept a return to military rule in Nigeria. This opens the way for President Yar'Adua to address overdue electoral and other reforms to make Nigeria a more credible and effective democracy.

The Carter Center will encourage this process by offering our services if a political decision is made to develop acceptable laws and procedures that can offer honest elections and, of course, we will continue our health and agriculture work among the people of Nigeria.

LIBERIA

Among all African nations, Liberia has the closest ties to the United States. A brief history will explain why The Carter Center has spent so much time and effort in this nation on the coast of West Africa.

In 1822, freed slaves and their descendants began moving to Liberia to establish a republic. They spoke English, brought a knowledge of the government they had left behind, and referred to themselves as Americans. They considered themselves superior to the natives and refused to be integrated into African society. In 1847 the settlers, congregated along the Atlantic coast, declared the independence of the Republic of Liberia and formed a government that they dominated. The main coastal cities were Monrovia and Buchanan, named for American presidents. The national flag was similar to the Stars and Stripes, but with only one star.

There was mistrust and hostility between the "Americans" and the natives in the interior, and a sharp distinction in their economic status. There was a huge "sale" of land in 1926 to the American-owned Firestone Plantation (for ten cents an acre), to be used for the production of rubber. Not incidentally, the president of Liberia acquired 25,000 acres that were planted and tended by Firestone for his personal benefit.

My earliest visit to Liberia was in 1978, while I was president. I chose it because of its history and because Liberia's president, William R. Tolbert, was the leader of the

Baptist World Alliance, representing all the Baptists in the world. Two years later, in 1980, Tolbert and thirteen other top government leaders were assassinated by an insurrectionist sergeant, Samuel Doe. (Doe was the first Liberian head of state who was not a member of the America-Liberian elite.)

There was an unsuccessful coup attempt in 1985, and Doe's troops responded by killing more than two thousand civilians and jailing more than a hundred opposing politicians, including a woman leader, Ellen Johnson-Sirleaf. A civil war followed, and five years later Doe was ousted, killed, and mutilated. An interim government was established by the Economic Community of West African States (ECOWAS), which actually controlled only about 5 percent of the nation, a small area around the capital city of Monrovia. The rest of the country was dominated by various warlords, notably Charles Taylor.

This is when The Carter Center became involved, and our peace fellow Dayle Powell, Rosalynn, and I made several visits to Monrovia and into the interior, trying to promote peace that could nurture a democratic government. We visited one of the operating rubber plantations, and I was angry to see how the indigenous Liberians

227

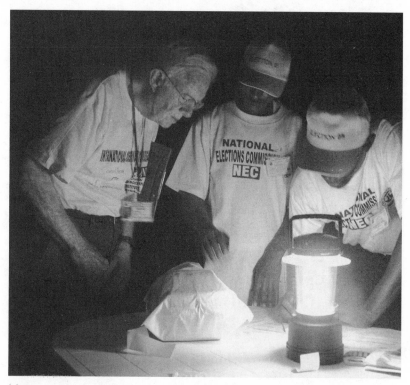

Votes were counted by lantern light in many polling stations throughout postconflict Liberia during the 2005 election witnessed by The Carter Center. (DEBORAH HAKES)

had been robbed of their lands and were still being treated almost as slaves. They lived in dormitories without windows and were forbidden to dig a hole in the ground. I published a poem about my observations, which aroused intense indignation from Firestone executives in America:

Why We Get Cheaper Tires from Liberia

The miles of rubber trees bend from the sea.
Each of the million acres cost a dime
nearly two Liberian lives ago.
Sweat, too,
has poured like sap from trees, almost free,
from men coerced to work by poverty
and leaders who had sold the people's fields.
The plantation kiln's pink bricks
made the homes of overseeing whites
a corporation's pride.
Walls of the same polite bricks divide
the workers' tiny stalls
like cells in honeycombs;
no windows breach the walls,
no pipes or wires bring drink or light
to natives who can never claim
this place as theirs
by digging in the ground.

No churches can be built,
no privy holes or even graves
dug in the rolling hills
for those milking Firestone's trees who die
from mamba and mosquito bites.

I asked the owners why.
The cost of land, they said, was high.

With pressure from the military arm of ECOWAS and to fulfill their political ambitions, the warlords were finally induced to turn in their weapons and disband their armies in order to qualify as candidates for the presidency. We examined a pile of 35,000 confiscated pistols, rifles, submachine guns, howitzers, and other guns (later dumped into the sea), and monitored the election in 1997. Ellen Johnson-Sirleaf was a strong candidate, but Charles Taylor prevailed in a technically honest and fair process, because he claimed to have governed his portion of the interior well and because people feared that fighting would resume if he lost.

We were prepared to help the new government, but despite the best efforts of our Center and others, the corrupt and despotic president persecuted his own people and incited conflict in neighboring countries. We decided to close our office in Monrovia after about three years because of human rights abuse, intimidation, and an environment that precluded discussion of government policies. Another rebellion began in 1999 and persisted for four years, bringing to more than 200,000 the number of people killed in the civil wars.

Finally, under great international pressure, Taylor abdicated and left for Nigeria, and The Carter Center joined the United Nations and others in helping with another Liberian election in 2005. Former president Nicéphore Soglo of Benin joined me as cochairman of our delegation, and the democracy experts David Carroll, Tom Crick, and Ashley Barr coordinated our efforts. More than 10 percent of the polling sites with an equivalent percentage of voters were officially deemed "difficult" or "inaccessible." No vehicles could reach them. It took hours and sometimes days to deliver voting materials by foot, horseback, or boat.

On Election Day, hundreds of people began lining up at polling sites soon after midnight, and there were enormous lines when polls opened officially at 8:00 A.M. Rosalynn and I visited forty-eight polling stations, all within the Monrovia area. The voters were surprisingly patient. There were many women with babies on their backs, some having been in line for more than ten hours before entering the voting booths. Election procedures were complex, but officials seemed to be well instructed and meticulous in performing their duties.

The results led to a runoff between Ellen Johnson-Sirleaf and the polling favorite, a famous soccer player named George Weah. By a substantial majority, the people chose Johnson-Sirleaf as their new leader, a Harvard-trained economist and the first woman president to be elected in Africa.*

Liberia is one of the most war-torn and poverty-stricken nations in the world, despite its rich natural resources in land, timber, and minerals. We have spent many days and nights in Monrovia. Except within foreign embassy compounds, all buildings have been damaged or destroyed. Fields are abandoned, there is astronomical unemployment, and most Liberians exist on less than fifty cents per day. When we visited Accra, Ghana, recently, Rosalynn said, "There is more difference in the quality of life between Monrovia and Accra than between

*Charles Taylor has been extradited from Nigeria and is facing multiple charges of war crimes and crimes against humanity before a special court in The Hague.

LIBERIANS PAVE THE ROAD TO DEMOCRACY

Once a schoolteacher, Jacob Lablah now teaches his fellow Liberians about the opportunities of democracy and the importance of voting. (DEBORAH HAKES)

Looking across the many rows of wood-and-mud shacks that house more than twelve thousand people in a camp for displaced persons in Margibi County, Liberia, Jacob Lablah knew he still had work to do. The scene inside the camp varied little from day to day. Women sat patiently next to stands selling combs, seasonings, and rice, while children carried toys made from tin cans and old plastic bottles, their shirts tattered and hanging off their shoulders. Men played checkers on a splintered wooden board for hours. People there had no jobs, no means to improve their lives, and no real place to call home.

Before the country's 2005 election, hundreds of thousands of Liberians lived in similar camps across the country, where Lablah worked to register voters and conduct civic education in preparation for Liberia's first national election in nearly ten years. Once a physics and math teacher, he decided to devote himself entirely to teaching civics to his fellow Liberians. Assisted by The Carter Center, he founded a grassroots organization called Promoting Activities for Development and Sustenance (PADS). He and his small staff educated voters in Margibi County's displaced persons camps, in high schools, and across the region's villages and towns.

The process has been difficult at times. Many Liberians were skeptical that their votes would matter or that an election could bring change. Their primary concern was not learning about government but getting food for their families, said Lablah. But he helped them realize that the democratic process is the means for improving the quality of life in Liberia.

Lablah's work involved not only instructing voters about how to fill out a ballot but also teaching residents the legal framework guiding elections and their human rights as Liberian citizens.

"We try to tell them that life is not yet finished," said Lablah. "We try to make them understand that if they aren't a part of selecting and electing their policy leaders, certainly there will be no change."

The persistent efforts of Lablah, PADS, and other Carter Center partners in Liberia paid off with high voter turnout for the 2005 elections. Monitors from the Center witnessed many Liberians waiting overnight in line to vote and others who walked for up to seven hours to reach their polling stations.

Once the historic election ended, Lablah continued to educate Liberians about their civic rights and responsibilities. "My greatest hope is sustaining a democracy," he said. "The election is not the

Liberians waited in long lones to vote for president. (DEBORAH HAKES)

end of the road. It's the beginning."

Two decades of commitment to Liberia began when our Center worked to foster peace during civil struggle in the early 1990s. Today, after successful elections, and with the support of a dynamic new president, Ellen Johnson-Sirleaf, the first elected female head of state in Africa, Liberians are determined to strengthen democracy with institutional and legal protections. The Carter Center has initiated a project to bring the legal system to rural areas and to incorporate traditional justice practices into new legal processes. Few people have suffered more or, at this moment, face more unprecedented opportunities for the alleviation of their suffering than Liberians.

Accra and New York."

The Carter Center is now working closely with Liberia's new president, and she has asked us to concentrate on substantive improvements in her nation's local and regional judicial processes. We hope to help establish a system that deals with strange and controversial subjects: whether there will be punishment for rape, whether husbands have the legal right to beat their wives and children, whether women can own property, whether witchcraft is a crime, and the legality of trial by ordeal.

Congo

When The Carter Center decided to observe the first democratic elections in the Democratic Republic of Congo, in 2006, there was general skepticism about whether a success would be possible in a country the size of Western Europe with only three hundred miles of roads. The nation was in a civil war and embroiled in a transitional political arrangement with different parts controlled by competing armed political factions. We believed that elections were the only way out of the deadly spiral — a means of legitimizing a government that could be held accountable. The safety of our monitors was uncertain, and we also were worried about whether any effort could succeed.

Under the leadership of UN Secretary-General Kofi Annan, the logistics were put in place for the most costly UN operation in history. Despite serious violence committed by some UN troops, the eighteen-thousand-member force was essential in stabilizing the volatile areas, but it was the determination and cooperation of the Congolese people that ultimately prevailed. The head of the Elections Commission, Apollinaire Malu Malu, brought exemplary leadership and commitment to transparency of the elections, and the hundreds of thousands of poll workers and police agents did their jobs well, despite the burning of polling stations and many other serious problems. Observers replaced the burned stations and all their necessary supplies and ballots.

The Carter Center fielded observers throughout the country, and our teams continued to face grave logistical challenges and political violence. Tragically, one of our fine observers, Guillaume Kakanou of Benin, lost his life, but the team persevered and continued to produce high-quality reports that became a principal resource for analysis of the process. The National Elections Commission accepted the recommendations from our reports, which helped to increase public confidence in the election process, which was completed in July 2006. A fragile peace is now prevailing in the troubled country, closely monitored by our Center.

CHAPTER FOUR
FIGHTING DISEASE

CLOSING THE GAP

There was a major turning point in the evolution of The Carter Center late in 1984, when we joined forces with Dr. William Foege to hold our first major consultation on health, entitled "Closing the Gap." Bill Foege was a leading epidemiologist who helped orchestrate the successful campaign to eradicate smallpox in the 1970s, became director of the U.S. Centers for Disease Control in 1977, and led in the formation of the Task Force for Child Survival & Development, a working group (including our Center) dedicated to immunization and other issues that enhance the quality of life for children around the world.

After eighteen months of preparation, about 120 experts assembled to assess the enormous gap between what is known about good health and what is actually done to utilize the available knowledge. We made it

President and Mrs. Carter have made dozens of trips to Africa to support the Center's work to prevent and eliminate unnecessary disease. They received the honor of wearing traditional garb during a visit to Tingoli village, northern Ghana, in 2007.
(LOUISE GUBB)

clear that we did not want theoretical discussions or dreams about the future, but concrete and practical information. The three main questions were these: What are the most prevalent causes of disease and death? How much of this morbidity and mortality can be prevented by using readily available knowledge? What can each of us do to stay healthier and live longer? The results were shocking. For instance, two-thirds of deaths before the age of sixty-five were found to be preventable, and fifty-year-old men or women who take well-known steps to reduce risk factors could add eleven years to their life span!

We used every possible means to promulgate the results of this analysis, including the publication of a book jointly written by Rosalynn and me entitled *Everything to Gain: Making the Most of the Rest of Your Life*. Several hundred thousand copies were sold, it remains in print, and I still sign the book as my later ones are published.

The Carter Center also developed a computer software system called the Health Risk Appraisal, to be used by individuals. By completing a computerized questionnaire concerning personal habits and medical history, we could obtain predictions of our own life expectancies. During the testing phase, groups of us would answer the questions together, and the software program would then let each of us know how our biological age compared to the years we had actually lived. There were some stunned silences and ashen faces among those who were obese, smoked cigarettes, got little exercise, or reported high cholesterol or blood pressure. A thirty-five-year-old man might learn that he had the life expectancy of an average person of fifty-three. In other words, he was forfeiting seventeen years of his potential life. He could then offer to lose thirty pounds, or give up smoking, and be told how many more years he might live. This program was soon adopted by universities, corporations, insurance companies, and other organizations interested in improving health. The concept is now used widely throughout the world. Since Rosalynn is a stickler for proper diet, neither of us has ever smoked, and we take a lot of exercise, our own results were very encouraging.

I never told the others that I was undergoing experimental medical procedures because of my high risk of cancer. My father had died of pancreatic cancer in his late fifties, and in the 1980s my two sisters, my brother, and my mother all succumbed to cancer, three of the cases proven to be in the pancreas. Probably because I was a famous person, this previously unknown familial pattern aroused great interest in the medical community, and a worldwide search was mounted for other similar families. (One was found in Japan with three deaths from cancer of the pancreas.) Since only about one person in ten thousand dies from this disease in the United States, the high incidence in our family defied mathematical odds — unless there was a genetic or familial cause. I agreed to undergo definitive physical examinations every three months in the hope that they might help lead to better information about the cause or early detection of pancreatic cancer.

In 1999 a prominent television executive named Marc Lustgarten died from pancreatic cancer, and a foundation was established bearing his name to promote research on and public awareness of the disease. I have helped the foundation with public service media spots, and recently they announced that medical scientists supported by them have discovered the first gene associated with cancer of the pancreas. So far, CAT and MRI scans and blood tests have not revealed that I have a problem. The only difference between me and the other members of my family is that all of them smoked cigarettes.

In addition to efforts related to Closing the Gap and the Health Risk Appraisal, my hatred of this deadly habit precipitated a desire for The Carter Center to support international efforts to reduce the threat of smoking. As a more enlightened public demanded increasing legal restraints on smoking in America, the unscrupulous tobacco manufacturers moved their propaganda focus to the unsuspecting and less informed people of the developing world. We called on Dr. John Hardman, a prominent Georgia psychiatrist, to represent us at the World Health Organization in Geneva in 1989 and 1990 to work on the first Global Initiative to Reduce Tobacco Use. Subsequently, John directed Rosalynn's mental health program, and then succeeded Dr. Bill Foege as executive director in 1992.

MENTAL HEALTH AFTER THE WHITE HOUSE
by Rosalynn Carter

The accomplishments of Rosalynn's mental health program, in themselves, have made the work of The Carter Center worthwhile.

— Jimmy Carter

When we lost the election in 1980, I thought I was coming home to Plains and would be

246

bored to death for the rest of my life. How wrong I was! The years since have been some of the most rewarding years of our lives. I truly regret that Jimmy did not win a second term. How much better off our country would be today if he had been reelected! But when I look forward and not back, I see that we probably never would have had The Carter Center, which has been a blessing to us and to many people around the world.

There were many things we had been working on in the White House that were important to us and for which we felt a responsibility. The Carter Center has given us a wonderful forum from which to continue to work on these and other issues. One of the best things for me about Jimmy having been president is that I can call on experts in any field, and almost without exception they will help me.

I am involved in all our Carter Center programs, but I have one special interest that is my own, and that is mental health. I worked hard on this issue from the governor's mansion in Georgia, and when I began campaigning for Jimmy for president, I had a chance to visit mental health programs all across our country. Word of my interest went ahead of me, and when I would arrive in a community, almost without exception, mental health advocates greeted me. If their needs were not being met, they wanted me to get help for them when my husband became president. If their program was good, they wanted to show it off. I saw very few good ones.

Less than a month after he was inaugurated, Jimmy announced the President's Commission on Mental Health. During the next four years, we worked hard investigating, recommending, and legislating a comprehensive mental health program. One of its lasting contributions was a tremendous increase in support for fundamental research, which has made a dramatic difference in our knowledge of the brain and mental illnesses. The centerpiece of the program was the Mental Health Systems Act of 1980, which was passed and funded — the first major reform of publicly funded federal mental health programs in years. Our celebration was brief, though, because the incoming president abandoned our legislation. I was devastated.

Although our first plan for The Carter Center was to resolve conflicts, it was inevitable that we would also establish a mental health program. It was with the help of a few key people with whom I had worked in the White House, and with whom I still work, that The Carter Center Mental Health Program came about. These include: Dr. Thomas Bryant, Chairman, President's Commission on Mental Health, 1977–78; Kathryn Cade, my projects director in the White House; Dr. Jeffrey Houpt, Dean, School of Medicine, Emory University; Dr. William Foege, Director, Centers for Disease Control, 1977–83, and Executive Director of The Carter Center, 1986–92; and Dr. Julius Richmond, Surgeon General of the United States and Assistant Secretary of Health and Human Services, 1977–81.

By 1985 we had raised enough funds to begin an annual symposium on mental health policy, which is now in its twenty-second year. The first subject we addressed was "stigma and the mentally ill." (Now I would say "people with mental illnesses.") We learned that those with mental illnesses are members of a minority group often defined in the news media not by their numbers but by denial to them of full and equal rights, opportunities, and power. Our goal was to marshal the efforts of many organizations to provide fairness, dignity, and more equitable distribution of resources to all people with mental illnesses.

Since stigma runs through every issue in the mental health field, the goal of eliminating stigma would be integral to any discussion we would have. Stigma is the issue on which I have focused the most time and effort, for it holds back progress in the entire field: attention from elected officials, funding for programs, the persistence of myths and misconceptions about the illnesses and those who live with them. And, very important, stigma keeps people from seeking help for fear of being labeled "mentally ill."

Our programs grew rapidly in number and in reputation, and it was obvious that we needed a director and a task force of individuals well versed in mental health matters to guide our work. Dr. John Hardman became our first director, and the members of our task force (established in 1991) were the very best in the field.

In addition to John Hardman, three others have led the mental health program: Dr. John Gates, formerly the Georgia State Director of Mental Health, Mental Retardation and Substance Abuse Services; Dr. Greg Fricchione, who had been Director of the Medical Psychiatry Service at Brigham and Women's Hospital in Boston, and also Director of Research for the Mind/Body Medical Institute. While here, he was also an Associate Professor of Psychiatry at the Harvard Medical School. Each of these individuals made his own special contribution, reflecting his particular area of interest. The current director is Dr. Thomas Bornemann. Before coming to The Carter Center, Thom served as senior adviser for mental health at the World Health Organization, and his leadership has been particularly helpful in our efforts to promote mental health as an integral part of disaster preparedness. He was called by our government to help victims of Hurricane Katrina deal with the traumas of that tragedy.

Our annual symposia have become important events in the mental health field. Each year they bring together leaders to address the most pressing concerns affecting those who live with mental illnesses. These leaders include representatives of the major mental health organizations, state and national officials, policy experts, advocates, consumers of mental health services, and family members. It has been particularly rewarding to have all the different mental health organizations meet together. Funding for mental health programs has always been so short that each group has had to grasp for what they could get for their own programs, so historically there has been more competition than collaboration among them. Yet these leaders come together at The Carter Center and work harmoniously on issues common to us all.

Like other Carter Center programs, our mental health conferences are action-oriented. At each symposium we develop a series of recommendations that the participants can pursue in their communities, in their states, or nationally, as their capacity allows. Perhaps most important to our participants are the partnerships with like-minded government agencies, nonprofit organizations, and influential individuals that develop during the meetings.

The symposia have covered many issues, including mental health among children and adolescents; parity in insurance coverage between mental and physical illnesses (perhaps the single most important policy effort); inclusion of mental health in government health care reform; mental health services in disaster and terrorism preparedness; mental health considerations in primary care; mental illness and the elderly; financing of mental health services; and family coping. When there has been a current topic of importance for the mental health community, we have covered it. Often the most poignant moments of our gatherings are the presentations from consumers, the real-life stories of those we are trying to help.

Through the symposia, we have been fortunate also to hold the first professional meetings to explore the findings of recent milestone reports: in 1999, it was Dr. David Satcher's first-ever Surgeon General's report on Mental Health; in 2000–2001, we discussed the two supplemental reports — "Culture, Race, and Ethnicity" and "Report of the Surgeon General's Conference on Children's Mental Health: A National Agenda"; in 2003 our program addressed the report of the President's New Freedom Commission, "Achieving the Promise: Transforming Mental Health Care in America"; and in 2005, The Institute of Medicine study, "Improving the Quality of Health Care for Mental and Substance-Use Conditions," was featured.

All of these were significant to the field. The surgeon general's report focused public attention on the issue when it stated that mental health is integral to everybody's health. The New Freedom Commission reported that the mental health system in our country is in a shambles. We have to start over and transform the whole system. And the symposium that featured the Institute of Medicine study was a first for us, bridging the mental health and substance-abuse communities. Mental health and substance-abuse officials and advocates have not always worked together (though Betty Ford and I have lobbied together for the two causes), and we have competed for years for funding. But at this symposium we had great discussions about the issues and learned how we could cooperate.

The Carter Center Mental Health Program has always reached out beyond our field to bring in participants. For instance, Mayor Rudolph Giuliani and representatives from the Department of Homeland Security were included in our 2002 program, "Meeting the Mental Health Needs of the Country in the Wake of September 11." And the same year we brought in juvenile justice system officials to discuss the problems of children and adolescents.

Each symposium sets goals and strategies for the participating organizations. For us at The Carter Center, that means public awareness through events, publications, interviews, or opinion pieces. Our advocacy efforts include communicating directly with members of Congress, testifying before committees, meeting with members of presidential commissions, or creating a program to deal with one crucial element of mental health.

The most significant and exciting program

has been the Rosalynn Carter Fellowships for Mental Health Journalism. Since the media have such a profound impact on what people think about mental illnesses and those who live with them, we decided that educating journalists so they could report more accurately on this subject would be the best way to change public attitudes and combat the negative effects of stigma.

Beginning in 1996, we have given annual stipends to as many as six American journalists to work on mental health issues, and in 2001 we expanded the program to include stipends for two journalists from New Zealand. Now we are working with journalists in southern Africa, with plans to expand to Romania this year. To date we have awarded seventy-eight fellowships to journalists representing radio, television, newspapers, magazines, and professional publications.

Our journalists have received much recognition for their work. The first year, one was honored by Amnesty International for an article on the treatment of mentally ill people in our country's jails. Another was nominated for an Emmy for her documentary on suicide. Others have received awards and nominations for Emmys and Pulitzer Prizes.

Other organizations, including the National Alliance on Mental Illness and Mental Health America, have begun programs that recognize and reward accurate reporting of mental health issues, and we have worked closely with the Columbia University School of Journalism on some efforts.

The Rosalynn Carter Chair in Mental Health at Emory University represents an important commitment to the integration of mental health into public health. The Rosalynn Carter Georgia Mental Health Forum is patterned after our national symposia, except that its focus is within our own state. Recognizing the need to promote mental health around the world, in 1992 the World Federation for Mental Health asked me to recruit first ladies in other countries to become involved. The International Committee of Women Leaders for Mental Health now includes first ladies and two queens, Noor of Jordan and Fabiola of Belgium. These leaders are extremely influential and are realizing great improvements in mental health care in their nations.

Our latest project is an initiative to encourage increased emphasis on mental health training for all medical students and to foster greater competency among primary care physicians in identifying and treating mental illnesses, especially depression. This program holds great promise for getting help for people before they are in crisis.

In addition to these activities, we have another opportunity to educate people about mental health issues through "Conversations at The Carter Center." We take turns with other Carter Center programs, inviting the public to join in exciting discussions about our work. One of our most effective sessions was an evening with Rod Steiger and Kathy Cronkite (Walter Cronkite's daughter), who talked about their own experiences with mental illness. A video of the event, narrated by Joanne Woodward, was distributed to more than 3,000 individuals and organizations and to 4,200 Blockbuster video stores throughout the country, made available to customers free of charge. (It is still available through the Mental Health Program.)

As mentioned earlier, one of our most important challenges is to get legislation passed requiring insurance coverage for mental illnesses on a par with that of other illnesses. We have had enough pledged votes in Congress since 2001 but have not been able to get bills out of committees because of misinformation about costs and concerns among insurers that health care expenditures will greatly increase. We in the mental health field know differently. For years we have collected statistics from companies and state governments that have full health coverage for their employees. Over time, the increase in their health costs is negligible, and data from the Congressional Budget Office show that, with the federal government covering all federal employees, the cost of providing parity for mental health and substance abuse in the Federal Employees Health Plan showed an increase of less than 1 percent. This study represents persuasive evidence that parity is indeed feasible and won't "break the bank."

Providing parity in insurance is crucial because many people do not seek treatment for mental illnesses because they can't afford it or because of the stigma attached. The best thing we can do to overcome stigma is to pass parity legislation. We will never stop striving for this goal.

I have seen a lot of progress in the thirty-five years I have spent working on mental health issues, but there is still much work to be done. The Carter Center Mental Health Program gives us a great opportunity to help reduce the stigma and discrimination that remain and to make life better for people who are experiencing mental illnesses.

Guided by our health consultant Dr. Don Hopkins, Rosalynn and I traveled as far as we could in our four-wheel-drive vehicles over a Ghanian road that had rarely known anything other than humans and animals on foot. Fortunately, it was during the dry season, in March 1988, and we could avoid the axle-deep ruts and bogs that would make the route impassable a few weeks later. We were about three hours from Ghana's capital, Accra, on the way to observe the human ravages of a disease that we had pledged to eradicate from the face of the earth: dracunculiasis, or Guinea worm.

Along with our companions from The Carter Center, we walked the rest of the way to our destination, a village of about five hundred people — almost as large as our hometown of Plains. These people could not converse with their nearest neighbors because they did not speak the same language, but the villages in the area had one thing in common: they had suffered for hundreds of years from this affliction.

When we arrived at an opening in the foliage, we saw several hundred people sitting or lying on the ground in the shade of the surrounding trees. We were quickly led to one group, who were sitting on woven mats or animal skins, obviously the most distinguished leaders of the community. None of them stood as we approached, but we noticed that all eyes were focused on one older man, quite small, stooped, and holding an ornate staff. A bright-colored woven robe, as thick as a blanket, was around his shoulders, and a floppy turban fitted low on his head. I had been told that, within his small domain, he had rarely met anyone who was considered of higher political stature than himself. A path opened as I walked toward him, with my head bowed and hands together in a demonstration of respect for his status. Regal but less than five feet tall, he rose to shake my hand, mumbled a few words that I could not understand, and then sat back down.

In African countries whose official language is French or Portuguese, there is always a three-step conversation, but since Ghana is an Anglophone country, I had to use only one interpreter as the chief and I exchanged the proper welcoming remarks. The other members of our party were directed to large overstuffed chairs, leaving the largest one vacant for my later use, while I explained the purpose of our visit. Rosalynn took out her stenographer's pad to make notes.

I began, "We understand that many people in your village have worms coming from their bodies, and we have come to give you some help in solving this problem. Our people will do nothing to interfere in your lives, and we will always seek your approval in advance. Can you tell me what you know about this disease?"

The chief stood before responding. "We are grateful that you are here to help us. I had heard that you were coming. Most of us are cursed with these worms, and we have assembled some of them here for you to see. Some others are too disabled to drag themselves from their huts, but you are welcome to visit them if you wish."

"Chief, do you know what causes this disease?"

"Some say the worms come from the blood of the wrong goats or sheep, others say the conjunction of the planets, and there are those among us who believe that this is a punishment by the gods for our sins."

"Have you ever heard that the worms come from the water that you drink?"

"No, this has never been told to me."

"I understand that the water in your village pond is precious to you, but it has tiny eggs in it that grow during a year's time into the adult worms that emerge. When suffer-

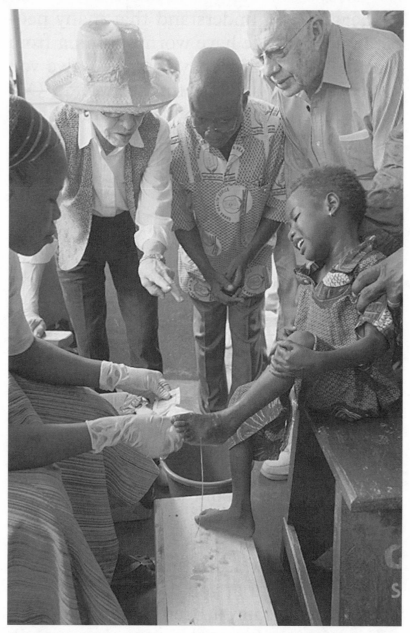

President and Mrs. Carter console a child as a health worker carefully winds a Guinea worm around a stick to coax it slowly out of her foot. (LOUISE GUBB)

ers wade into the pond to alleviate their pain or to dip up more water, the female worms lay countless eggs, which repeat the cycle."

The chief was obviously upset to hear this, and he and his associates had a spirited discussion before he responded.

"We can look at the water and we see no worms. Our water hole is sacred to us. It always fills during the rainy season and sustains us throughout the year. If it were not here, we would have no village, and our revered ancestors would not have lived."

I did my best to convince the chief that my facts were accurate but that they implied no negative reflection on the character or integrity of the pond. Nevertheless, these foreign larvae were injected into the pure and perhaps holy water by these vicious worms, an insult to their ancestors. Our purpose was to work with the villagers to remove this contamination from their water before it went into their mouths.

After more consultation, there was a somewhat reluctant agreement that we could proceed with our attack on the worms. We were then invited to move around the large circle of villagers, with those suffering from Guinea worm having been placed in the front. They constituted more than half of the total population. Just at a glance, we could see that the thin white worms were emerging from various parts of the bodies, many of them from between the toes, from feet and ankles, and out of arms and legs. Others were concealed by people's clothing. Each worm had caused great swelling around its exit point, and we noticed worms that had been wrapped around sticks about the size of a pencil. Some of the people were obviously in excruciating pain. Many small children wept quietly.

I noticed one beautiful young woman standing near the edge of the crowd, apparently holding a baby in her right arm. Thinking that this might be the youngest sufferer of all, I went to see this special case. As I approached, I saw that she was holding not a baby but her grossly swollen right breast, with a Guinea worm coming from the nipple. (Later, I was told that the same girl had eleven other worms emerge from her body.) I fought back tears. After slowly circling the open area, stopping to console the suffering victims or to consult with Don Hopkins, the world's foremost expert on the disease, we visited some of the small huts to examine the cases. Worms in a person's crotch or in knee joints were especially troublesome. Muscle tissue in children was often so severely damaged by the large sores

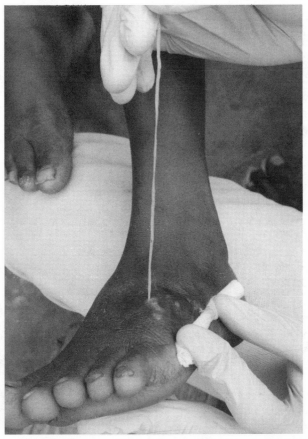

Guinea worms are thin, threadlike parasites that can grow up to three feet long. The worm is known as the "fiery serpent" for causing burning blisters as it exits the skin gradually, in one to three months. (Louise Gubb)

Villagers gather water from a Guinea worm–infested pond in Savelugu, Ghana. (Louise Gubb)

that the permanent aftereffects were similar to those of polio.

Don Hopkins was the unchallenged hero of our group. He had been closely associated with Dr. Bill Foege in the eradication of smallpox in 1977 and was then in charge of our Center's program to eradicate the world's second disease, Guinea worm. Don was later awarded a MacArthur "genius" award and knighted by the nation of Mali. In Africa he was known as the Redeemer of Less Privileged and was an honorary chief in several regions. Don is now the vice president of The Carter Center and head of all our health programs.

Having been instructed by Dr. Hopkins, all of our team knew that dracunculiasis is a disease known since biblical times that plagues people who obtain their drinking water from a stagnant pond. Microscopic in size, the Guinea worm's larvae are imbibed by a small water flea or cyclops that can be seen in clear water with a simple magnifying glass. The next mandatory stage in its evolution is within a human body; sheep, goats, or other animals cannot fulfill this requirement. This means that, if the human phase of this cycle can be completely broken, Guinea worm can be controlled or eliminated from a pond. The problem is that no villager can wade into the water when adult female worms are prepared to squirt out hundreds of thousands of fresh larvae. Before being imbibed, every drop of water must pass through a fine filter cloth to remove the water fleas. Residents of every village must comply with these strict restraints for a full year. We explained these facts to the chief of the village and to his companions and the other villagers who could hear our voices.

Then the chief spoke again: "We have to drink the water from this pond or perish. There is no other source for us."

I replied, "We will give your people a fine cloth, through which they must pour every drop of the water before it is consumed. Everyone in the village must do this for an entire year. If no one wades into the pond with a Guinea worm, then there will be no eggs in the future to infect your water. If you choose a few trustworthy people, we will give them the filter cloths to distribute and teach them how they must be used."

Rosalynn and I and other representatives of The Carter Center went to thousands of communities where Guinea worm was found. When our first national survey of Ghana was complete, we had identified 179,000 cases of the disease in 6,515 villages. This proved to be the second-most endemic country, with Nigeria assuming the lead with 660,000 cases in 5,879 villages. Our task in these two nations and in eighteen others — three in Asia and fifteen in sub-Saharan Africa — was to visit every indigenous community and teach the people what they could do to end the vicious cycle of pain and suffering. With an estimated 3.6 million cases found in more than 23,600 villages, this would be quite a task. (For several years we could not visit a large area of Southern Sudan because of an ongoing civil war.)

Our first knowledge of Guinea worm had come with a visit to The Carter Center in 1986 by Dr. Peter Bourne, a physician and anthropologist who had been my adviser when I was governor of Georgia on combating drug problems, primarily addiction to heroin, at that time. As president, I appointed Peter to be my special assistant for health issues and to hold the newly created position of director of drug control policy (the nation's first "drug czar"). Subsequently, he became an assistant secretary-general at the United Nations, where he established and ran the International Drinking Water Supply and Sanitation Decade, which promoted the availability of clean drinking water throughout the world and dealt with diseases caused by unclean water.

When Peter came to see us, he showed slides of what he considered the most obnoxious and neglected of all waterborne diseases, depicting worms emerging in various places from people's bodies. I accepted his challenge that our Center study the problem, and we immediately obtained definitive information from the nearby Centers for Disease Control and Prevention. Guided by Dr. Hopkins, that same year we adopted the complete eradication of this disease as our first major health project.

In addition to having villagers enforce the restraints I had explained to the Ghanaian village chief, another task was to prevent strangers or visitors from contaminating the village water supply. One additional help is a commercial pesticide (ABATE®) that can be poured into smaller infected water holes to kill the worms and their host cyclops. But this is easier said than done.

The citizens in endemic Guinea worm villages are often the poorest, most isolated and neglected people on Earth. They do not live near running streams or have water wells, and their entire lives are spent within easy walking distance of the local rain-fed water hole. They know from generations of experience that there is no effective treatment for the disease except to put a slight tension on the emerging worm in order to expedite its painful exit by a few days. If the worm is accidentally broken, the dead and rotting portion left in the body can cause a potentially fatal infection. Unfortunately, even those few who had learned about the use of filter cloths had been frustrated because the finest known fabrics would rot quickly if wet and dried a dozen times during a tropical day.

We knew that to accomplish the huge task of eradication of this disease in India, Pakistan, and Yemen plus seventeen African nations would be very expensive and difficult. Just one of the endemic countries, Sudan, was larger than all the combined American states east of the Mississippi River. As The Carter Center's chief fund-raiser, I had the job of obtaining financial support for our project, and I explained the facts about Guinea worm repeatedly to potential donors in nations around the world. We hit a gold mine on one of my first forays to New York City, when I visited a longtime friend, Edgar Bronfman. He and I met for lunch at his office, and I explained the purpose of my visit, being careful to avoid describing the most nauseating aspects of the disease. Then I asked him to contribute fifty thousand dollars each year for five years.

He immediately agreed, and then asked how the money would be spent. I replied that villagers needed to pour their water through filter cloths, similar to the table napkins we were using. I added that the cloths would have to be replaced at least once or twice during the year because the fabric would rot. Edgar informed me that he and his family owned a substantial portion of the stock in DuPont, and he offered to see if the company's scientists could develop a special fiber that would resist rotting.

Within a few months, this had been accomplished, and DuPont contracted with Precision Fabrics Group to weave the cloth for us. When Rosalynn and I visited the textile factory in Roanoke, Virginia, I learned that they specialized in the production of finely woven cloth for uses such as typewriter ribbons, parachutes, and bulletproof vests. Whenever two fibers crossed, they were welded together so they wouldn't slip or spread. Ultimately, DuPont contributed to our project more than 2 million square meters of this precious cloth! This would prove to be the key to our success.

Since I needed to visit Southwest Asia late in 1986 on other Center business, Pakistan was the first endemic country on our agenda. I had known General Muhammad Zia-ul-

Haq when we both served as presidents, and he listened intently when I explained our interest in ridding his nation of Guinea worm — with which he was not familiar. He agreed to send one of his top generals to The Carter Center to spend two weeks in intensive study of eradication procedures and gave him full government backing when he returned. In 1993, Pakistan became the first country to report the last indigenous case, and within five more years this achievement was equaled by Kenya, India, Senegal, Yemen, Cameroon, and Chad. Since then, Central African Republic, Uganda, Mauritania, and Benin have been added to the list.

One basic policy of The Carter Center is to depend on natives in a country to do the work among their fellow citizens. This gives us a tremendous advantage in using our limited funds more efficiently and magnifying the effectiveness of a relatively small number of skilled employees. The normal policy of most large international agencies is to send into the capital city of a developing nation a small staff, perhaps ten or a dozen people, rent a few rooms, buy some vehicles and install telephones, and then begin working with the appropriate government minister. Having been president of a great nation, I can short-circuit this procedure.

In advance, I notify the king, president, or prime minister that I intend to make a visit, usually with my wife and a small entourage. The head of state is informed of our major purpose: to help eradicate Guinea worm, to reduce the incidence of onchocerciasis, or to increase production of food grains. I request that we be permitted to meet with all the ministries that might be involved, which usually include health, education, finance, transportation, agriculture, and water supplies. After a large welcoming ceremony at the airport, we soon are able to describe our entire project, which leads to an official contract, or "Memorandum of Understanding," between the nation and The Carter Center. Working always under government officials and with no authority of our own, we agree to provide one of the world's most noted experts on the subject, who will train key workers throughout the country. We will also furnish all the needed supplies, such as filter cloths, special medicines, optimum varieties of seeds for the latitude and altitude, plus a limited number of vehicles, from pickup trucks to bicycles. Only in rare cases do we pay the local workers or their supervisors a per diem, never a salary.

One additional stratagem (with which Rosalynn and others have disagreed) is that we try to refrain from putting our name on the projects. It doesn't belong to Jimmy Carter or The Carter Center. We have used the name Global 2000, so that a village chief or a head of state can take credit for any success by saying, "My Global 2000 project eradicated Guinea worm," or "Our G2000 program increased maize production by 60 percent last year." Also, we make sure that our limited funds and supplies go directly to fulfill our goals and not to government agencies or the ubiquitous American contractors who absorb a good portion of foreign-aid funds.

One serious problem that we faced in the eradication of Guinea worm was that few if any of the adults in extremely remote villages were literate, and often there were no radios or television. How could the crucial information be disseminated to *every* citizen in *every* village? After some troubling delays, we finally learned to use cartoons to tell our story. We created teaching posters in which there would be two women standing in a shallow pond and dipping up water. The first woman would be pouring the water through a filter cloth, drinking the water, and remaining healthy and happy. The second woman would drink her water without using a filter, and the next frame would show her grimacing in pain and looking at a Guinea worm emerging from her leg.

As in our peace programs, we have recruited top political leaders in promoting our efforts to control diseases. I arranged to have a personal meeting with President Alpha Oumar Konaré when I visited Mali in 1992 to promote the eradication of Guinea worm. As a courtesy, I was met at the airport by General Amadou Toumani Touré, who had recently stepped down from the presidency to permit free democratic elections. As we rode together, he asked about the main purpose of my trip and was surprised to learn that a former president of the United States would deign to involve himself in the eradication of a relatively unknown disease. His mother had been expelled from high school because Guinea worms had caused her to miss so many classes. He volunteered immediately to join The Carter Center in this effort and came to Atlanta for intensive instruction before becoming our roving ambassador in all the endemic Francophone nations.

We had reached something of a stalemate in Nigeria, where hundreds of thousands of Guinea worm cases persisted, when General (and former president) Yakubu Gowon adopted the disease's eradication as his personal project. He visited many endemic communities and used persuasion and public news media to shame, cajole, and convince public officials and private citizens to take action. By the end of 2006, there were only forty-two cases in the entire country, all in one small community where we are now concentrating our efforts.

Among our many partners, Peace Corps volunteers proved especially effective. In some heavily endemic African nations, almost half the volunteers would be assigned to this task. Like all the rest of us, some of them faced times of frustration. We met two young women volunteers stationed in a village in arid northern Niger where Guinea worms had prevented any planting of crops that season. To tell the necessary story, they had drawn cartoons of the two women standing in a shallow pond. The villagers were outraged when they saw the pictures and protested, "We would rather have Guinea worms than no feet!"

Residents of many villages proved to be extremely innovative, often enhancing the contributions of our trained health workers. Very few of our assignees spoke any of the regional languages, and even health ministry officials rarely knew the local dialects, so the people composed songs with lyrics that described the Guinea worm cycle and what must be done to break it. We were frequently entertained by the performance of these songs and even elaborate stage plays, filled with drama and humor. We had our cartoon posters printed on cloth from which women made brightly colored dresses, and I was given several shirts emblazoned with the same motif.

We soon saw small sections of filter cloth sewn carefully into the tops of baseball caps or other head coverings — always available when busy people happened to become thirsty but weren't carrying the larger cloth that we furnished to each family in endemic villages. Ultimately one of the most helpful inventions originated among the Tuaregs, a nomadic people who live in the Sahara Desert of Africa, in the Guinea worm areas of northern Mauritania, Mali, and Niger. The men, who traditionally have worn indigo-colored turbans and veils, have a reputation as fearless fighters and pride themselves on their fine horses or camels. Unlike the villagers described earlier, these people have no local ponds or households but drink as they can from many water sources. We soon noticed that they were wearing short reeds hanging from their necks by strings, with tiny pieces of our filter cloth tied around the ends. In this way, they could ensure that every drop of imbibed water was carefully filtered. This invention was to prove invaluable in our most challenging country, Sudan.

Despite amazing success during the first few years of our effort, we learned that the eradication of the final few cases of Guinea worm disease in a nation can be delayed by complacency or carelessness, the arrival of itinerant workers who ignore a local village's rule against wading in a pond while adult worms are emerging, or the failure of a town's deep well or piped water system, which causes unprecedented use of an infected pond.

Sudan presented a special problem, at one point having about three-fourths of all the cases in the world. With a total population of 40 million, the nation has been divided by civil war for more than twenty years. There are seven provinces in the north ruled by the Islamic regime in Khartoum and three provinces in the south governed by a rebel group known as the Sudan People's Liberation Army/Movement (SPLA/M). The preeminent cause of the prolonged conflict has been the refusal of the non-Muslim southerners to accept the imposition of Islamic

Sharia law. Large regions comprising many villages and water holes in Southern Sudan remained inaccessible to our health workers because of sustained combat or almost impassable fields of land mines.

When all other efforts failed, in 1995 Rosalynn and I attended a multinational conference in Khartoum on Guinea worm eradication. First, however, we flew to Nairobi to meet with the SPLA/M leader, John Garang. He had earned a doctorate in agricultural economics from Iowa State University and was an intelligent and charismatic leader. I had known him for many years, beginning on a Sunday morning in the mid-1980s when he and four of his associates had come unexpectedly into my Bible class in our home church in Plains. Subsequently during our visits in Africa, he and I discussed the lesson I'd been teaching that day, about Joshua's leadership of the Hebrew people after the death of Moses.

Garang was deeply concerned about the prevalence of Guinea worm throughout the region he governed, and he offered to help provide access to as many additional communities as possible. He and I examined his most detailed maps, and it soon became evident that this goal could be reached only if both armies declared a cease-fire. There was an apparently insurmountable tactical obstacle concerning the seasons of the year. The northern army, with its tanks and other motorized vehicles, had a clear advantage in mobility during the dry months, whereas Garang's guerrilla fighters were much more effective during the rainy season, when the roads were impassable and the intricate waterway system was full or overflowing.

After obtaining Garang's commitment to the concept of a cease-fire, but only during the dry months, we flew to Khartoum to attend the regional conference and meet with the Sudanese president, Omar al-Bashir. I had known him for several years, before he overthrew the previous leaders in a military coup in 1989, and I was certain he would insist that most of the Guinea worm problem was in the south and therefore Garang should make the tactical concession and permit any cease-fire to last only during the rainy season. I also knew that Bashir was suffering from a bad image in the Western world and that recent congressional testimony had revealed our government's desire to overthrow the Khartoum regime. Our only hope for concessions lay in the advantages of positive public relations, so I persuaded the African CNN crew headquartered in Nairobi, headed by Gary Streiker, to accompany us to Sudan.

At the Khartoum airport, I was informed that Bashir preferred my first meeting be with his minister of security, Nafi'e Ali Nafi, and his minister of state, Salah al-Din Ghazi, two charismatic young men with doctoral degrees from American universities. They made it plain to me that there would be no cease-fire during the dry season, and I responded that it was obvious they were committed only to a military option and were callous about suffering in the south. I pointed out that Sudan was widely blamed for the continuing war and the subversion of its neighbors, appeared insensitive to human rights, was becoming more isolated, and might become another Iran or Iraq. I pointed out that positive moves were necessary to engender better relations with the United States and other Western nations. The ministers expressed surprise and strong disapproval at my comments and added that these were all allegations that had been promulgated by the U.S. government to destroy their nation's reputation. I told them there was no reason for us to discuss matters further, and as they were leaving I mentioned that I had brought the CNN crew with me in the hope that some positive news might be generated during my visit.

In our subsequent meeting, President Bashir had obviously been briefed about my meeting with his ministers. He was more diplomatic, grateful for our longtime interest in Sudan and for our mediating peace talks in 1989, for our project that had quadrupled the nation's wheat production, and our health efforts in the north. However, he was not forthcoming on my cease-fire proposal. He claimed that a cease-fire was not badly needed since 90 percent of the south could be reached within areas controlled by his government forces. After the meeting, Rosalynn and I observed that Dr. Ghazi had been quite influential, interrupting or even correcting the president on occasion, very quietly and without apology.

The next morning, after Rosalynn and I had jogged along the confluence of the Blue and White Nile rivers, Dr. Ghazi came to discuss with us plans for the regional Guinea worm conference scheduled for later that morning. Our meeting soon developed an unanticipated intensity. He reiterated his government's opposition to a cease-fire, claiming that it would just give Israel, Uganda, Eritrea, and others more time to rearm the rebels. I replied that many Americans were becoming convinced that Sudan was not interested in peace or in the well-being of citizens in the south, who were not Muslims.

Somewhat angry, I informed Ghazi that this would be my last visit to Khartoum and I planned to announce at an afternoon press conference that my efforts to convince the government had failed and that Sudan had chosen the military option in lieu of any move toward peace or the alleviation of suffering. Also, Rosalynn and I would cancel plans for further Carter Center projects in Sudan, including sending one of our sons to ensure good-faith observation of the cease-fire by both the north and the south. We noticed that Ghazi paid close attention to this last remark.

At the Guinea worm conference, attended by several hundred Sudanese and foreign officials and with Bashir presiding, I made a strong speech emphasizing the great problem with suffering in the south from several preventable diseases. I analyzed the necessity for a cease-fire and emphasized that (a) it was not to be used to build up forces, (b) there would be unbiased condemnation of any violations, (c) it would begin immediately and last two months during the dry season but I would strive to extend it throughout the coming rainy season, (d) our Center would ensure unimpeded communication with Khartoum, and (e) I would personally guarantee these commitments by sending our son Chip to work between the northern and southern regions. As the conference adjourned, Minister Ghazi informed me that President Bashir would be meeting with his military commanders and would give me a final answer at 5:00 P.M. I told him I would have to leave Khartoum at 8:00 P.M., after holding a press conference with the international news media.

Later that afternoon, I was informed that Bashir would join me at the press conference and would make a positive statement. He declared a unilateral cease-fire to begin the next day at midnight and to continue for two months, hoping that Garang and the SPLA/M would respond favorably. He also announced a general amnesty for all those who had fought against the government during the past twelve years and made a strong plea for a united Sudan. I thanked him for his generosity and reported that we had a pledge from Japan for immediate delivery of a fleet of vehicles to make it possible for our health workers to reach as many communities as possible during the cease-fire. Our access to Southern Sudan was subsequently extended to almost six months, including part of the rainy season, and this was the turning point in eradicating Guinea worm. Craig Withers, an expert on Guinea worm disease, was transferred from Nigeria to Sudan to take advantage of this opportunity.

We made great progress during this brief time of peace but were faced with a quandary when the intense fighting resumed. By this time, Dr. Ernesto Ruiz-Tiben had become the director of our Guinea Worm Eradication Program, and he remembered the Tuaregs and their reed filters. We turned to a Norwegian NGO, Health and Development International, which substituted a six-inch length of plastic PVC piping for the reed and commissioned women workers in Nairobi to produce nine million of the pipe filters, with instructions for use inserted inside each pipe. With John Garang's support, these were distributed to villagers throughout the inaccessible war zones. After a comprehensive peace agreement was adopted in 2005, we finally conducted a more complete survey in Southern Sudan, reaching about three thousand villages for the first time. We were pleased to find that the pipe filters and other efforts since the "Guinea worm cease-fire" had been effective, and we found a total of only 20,383 cases of Guinea worm remaining from a much larger estimate ten years earlier.

The second-largest number of cases remains in Ghana, where we had a serious disappointment late in 2005, when a turbine pump in the northern region of Ghana that provided water to the large town of Savelugu and some surrounding villages failed. Tragically, commercial water carriers sent their tanks to a local pond infested with Guinea worm larvae and sold the unfiltered water to unsuspecting families. This resulted in an outbreak a year later of several hundred cases, bringing Ghana's 2006 total to 4,136. We visited the region in February 2007 to assess the damage and to initiate extraordinary control procedures, including heavy treatment of ponds with ABATE® and the stationing of guards at each water hole in the area to ensure the filtering of any water to be hauled away and sold. Ghanaian President John Agyekum Kufour and his administration pledged their total commitment to preventing further problems.

As I write this chapter, we are faced with remaining challenges only in Sudan and Ghana. Among the other eighteen nations that have addressed the disease, eleven reported no remaining cases during 2006, and the other seven had a total of 497, each of which was being carefully monitored and contained.

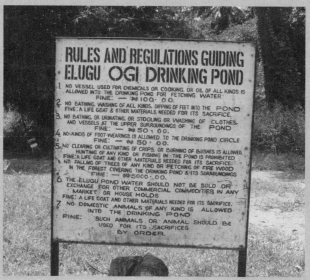

Community members in Elugu Ogi who do not follow the rules and regulations of the Sacred Pond are fined—cows, goats, yams, and kegs of palm wine. For example, water may not be sold; no one can bathe, fish, or urinate in the pond; and no domestic animals may enter it. Village chiefs eventually issued a fine to those who tried to prevent the use of ABATE® larvicide to prevent Guinea worm disease in the community.
(EMILY STAUB)

Stagnant ponds of water that form during the rainy season are worshipped as a source of life by many villagers in parched rural Nigeria. Yet, often unknown to them, these same ponds can perpetuate the horrible Guinea worm disease that afflicts their communities. Offering help in the face of such ingrained cultural beliefs requires our field staff to be resourceful.

When the Guinea worm eradication campaign began in Nigeria in 1988, there were more than 660,000 cases of the disease, more than in any country. Guinea worm is not fatal, but it can cripple, and the slow emergence of a long thin worm through the skin after it has developed inside the human body for a year causes a painful burning sensation and can destroy the surrounding muscle tissue. Entire communities can be stricken at once, destroying local economies.

Yet in the village of Elugu Ogi in Ebonyi State, when our field-workers arrived to apply safe larvicide that targets the parasite in the water, the women who gather water from the pond became outraged.

"They believed that if we treated the water, their gods, the spirits of the ancestors who protect the pond and watch over the village, would be destroyed," said Emmanuel Miri, Carter Center country representative. "We could not easily convince them that they get this disease from contaminated water. They thought it was a curse of their ancestors."

Miri knew the resistance would continue, so he recruited the former Nigeria head of state General Yakubu Gowon to talk to all of the village elders: the chief of the pond, the paramount chief, and the religious chief. Gowon, a respected African leader, has been key to sustaining the national momentum that has brought Guinea worm disease to the brink of eradication in his country.

"I told them that tradition is important, and that even if the soul of their ancestor is in the fish in the pond, the ABATE® larvicide would not kill any of the animals — fish, turtles, snakes — in the pond, and that it would be quite safe. I said the spirit of their ancestors would not like it if their children on Earth should suffer because of some kind of disease. They would not be good ancestors if they watch them die from such preventable circumstances," Gowon recounted.

The leaders soon agreed to have the pond treated, saying, "The ancestors are

A Nigerian girl collects water for her family at the Sacred Pond in Elugu Ogi, Ebonyi state. Since the pond was treated, there is no more Guinea worm disease. (EMILY STAUB)

good ancestors. They would not want us to suffer." But when the chiefs walked with General Gowon to the pond, they found the women had formed a human barrier around it. Their faces were colored red, and they chanted a song of resistance.

"There was a misstep," said Miri. "The women had not been consulted."

"I appealed to the women. I told them they should have been consulted and that the ABATE® would not harm the animals or the spirit of their ancestors," Gowon said. "Then I left the village, giving them time to talk among themselves."

The village council was furious and instituted a fine — cows, goats, yams, and kegs of palm wine — for refusing the treatment to the pond. They also sent a letter of apology to General Gowon.

The sacred pond of Elugu Ogi was treated several times. Guinea worm no longer exists in that village today, and only forty-two cases of the disease occurred throughout Nigeria in the year 2007. Little miracles like that one in 23,600 villages in twenty countries where the disease was initially endemic mean that someday soon a terrible and ancient disease will be wiped off the face of the earth.

GUINEA WORM WARRIOR FIGHTS AGAINST ALL ODDS

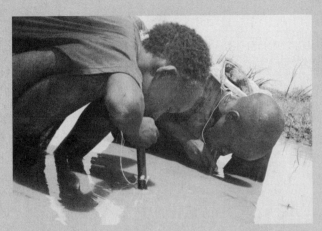

Sudanese boys use pipe filters to protect themselves from contracting Guinea worm disease. A filter on the end of the strawlike device strains out the waterborne parasite. (EMILY STAUB)

Some called him "The Great One." Living for a week on one small sack of supplies, getting food from people along the way, Abdelgadir El Sid became a legend among field-workers fighting disease in Africa.

In the 1970s, he earned his reputation by uncovering the last case of smallpox in a remote village in Somalia. Having been told that no one there had the disease, he suspected villagers might be reluctant to admit the presence of "a pox upon them" out of shame. So he created a commotion, purposely driving his jeep into a ditch, which attracted everyone in the village to witness the scene, including the last remaining victim of smallpox in the world.

Not one to rest, into his late sixties, he was again astonishing colleagues with his relentless pursuit of his objectives. This time Abdelgadir was helping The Carter Center eradicate Guinea worm disease in war-ravaged Southern Sudan, the region with the largest concentration of remaining cases.

Sudan is the greatest challenge to Guinea worm eradication, accounting for the majority of all remaining cases in 2007. During the summer of 2001, The Carter Center and its partners — Health & Development International, Hydro Polymers of Norsk Hydro, and Norwegian Church Aid — blanketed Sudan with more than nine million pipe filters, one for every man, woman, and child at risk of Guinea worm disease. This special project was necessary because of the continued conflict, the number of displaced and nomadic persons, and the difficulties of accessing safe drinking water and delivering household filters to every endemic home.

Southern Sudan has few miles of paved road and no electricity, yet eradicating Guinea worm calls for every village to be assessed and every infected village to be served. "The most difficult part," Abdelgadir said, "is just getting to remote endemic villages. Sometimes you have to sleep in the forest, get people to help pull your boat, and hope you can find someone to feed you during your journey."

The rainy season was the most challenging time: navigating swollen streams strewn with floating tree stumps, avoiding poisonous snakes, and simply finding one's way over altered courses in waterways. On one weeklong journey, Abdelgadir had to leave his boat and wade for eight hours in water sometimes up to his neck, carrying a bundle of cloth filters to a remote village where they could be used to strain Guinea worm larvae from drinking water.

"There was nowhere to rest that whole day. All I could see around me was water. But that wasn't the worst part," he said.

"I had to avoid rebel fighters, who might shoot you for no reason."

The 2005 peace accord among warring parties in Sudan renewed prospects that intrepid field-workers like Abdelgadir could reach many villages that were previously inaccessible due to the conflict, and we now see the real prospect that existing cases can be contained and eliminated forever.

RIVER BLINDNESS

As we devised a system to eradicate Guinea worm disease, it soon became obvious to us that other diseases could be controlled in some of the African nations. We would become acquainted with village leaders, recruit and train local health workers, devise methods for communicating in the local language, and — most important of all — demonstrate that a cooperative effort could alleviate suffering. Most often, onchocerciasis, or river blindness, would prove to be endemic to the same areas.

Our struggle against onchocerciasis really began with a remarkable demonstration of corporate generosity by Merck & Co., one of the major pharmaceutical companies.

"Oncho" is second only to trachoma as the world's leading infectious cause of blindness. Medical scientists have known for many years that the disease is caused by worms transmitted through the sting of a tiny black fly that breeds in turbulent streams, where the water has a high concentration of oxygen. Existing in six countries in Latin America and much more prevalent in Africa, oncho constitutes a serious obstacle to economic development, because for centuries people have moved away from streams and their adjacent fertile bottomlands to escape the flies.

Adult worms lodge in nodules under the skin and release into surrounding tissues large numbers of microfilaria (microscopic worms), which move through the body and, after dying, cause skin rashes, lesions, intense itching and depigmentation of the skin, general debilitation, and serious visual impairment and blindness.

A major effort was begun in 1974 to spray streams in eleven African countries to reduce the black fly populations, but this program was very expensive and only partially successful. In the 1980s, Merck scientists learned that their veterinary medicine Heartgard, used to protect pets and other animals from heartworms, could protect humans from onchocerciasis. The medicine's generic name is ivermectin, and the same medicine for humans would be called Mectizan®.

In 1988 Dr. Roy Vagelos, CEO of Merck, came to visit our executive director, Dr. Bill Foege, and offered to provide a substantial quantity of the medicine to us if we could evolve a protocol that would prevent the free pills from interfering with the sale of Heartgard. Once this was done, we and other nongovernmental organizations began delivering the pills to some of the endemic areas in Africa and placing them in the mouths of people in communities where oncho was rampant.

For a person of average size, one tablet was sufficient to control the microfilaria, but the adult worms have a life span of about fourteen years and remain alive. Annual treatments were required to control the intense itching and skin discoloration, and to prevent blindness. Delivery had to be tightly controlled because the tablets were extremely valuable to people with the disease; some said it would be a difficult choice between the Mectizan® and a diamond of the same size.

On one of our trips to Africa in 1994, we decided to go to southern Chad to visit a village ravaged by river blindness, to spend some time with Dr. Vagelos, and to make a film that could be used to help control the disease in other African countries where we were active. There were about five hundred people in the community, and almost all of them had oncho in some stage. In their eagerness to obtain the tablets, people in line were pressing against each other so closely that Rosalynn noted it would be impossible to put a newspaper between them. They were receiving from one-half to two tablets, depending on their measured size. Already, about 5 percent of the people in the village were totally blind, including a shocking number of young people.

A blind man is led by his son through their village. Thanks to distribution of the drug Mectizan®, his son may walk freely his whole life. (JEFF WATSON)

River blindness developed as a problem in this village when, in the early 1970s, the Chinese had built a dam to provide irrigation water for the rice crop. The dam created rapids suitable for the fly to breed, and subsequently the rice fields were abandoned and the dam opened to disperse the black flies. Dr. Vagelos and I stood on the dam in front of the video cameras so that our discussion of the disease could be recorded. With treatment of the people by Mectizan®, the irrigation pond could once more provide water for the rice crop, and the people could lead normal lives. To his surprise, I asked Dr. Vagelos if Merck would consider making a blanket offer of enough medicine to treat every endemic community in the world. He gulped, hesitated, laughed, and then replied that he would discuss my request with his company's board of directors.

This extraordinary commitment was soon made, and Merck has donated more than 530 million treatments since 1987, currently reaching more than 60 million people in Africa, Latin America, and Yemen each year.

During the early stages of the effort to combat river blindness, I was told that the high cost of delivering Merck's free pills to remote villages was financed by the River Blindness Foundation, but I didn't inquire about the origin of the funds. One day I went to Houston, Texas, to deliver the graduation address at Rice University and was introduced to a man sitting unobtrusively in a corner of the reception room. He was John Moores, and I soon learned that he and his wife, Becky, were the founders of the River Blindness Foundation, which was financed from their personal funds. Subsequently, John became involved in many of the other activities of The Carter Center, and in 2005 he succeeded me as chairman of our board of trustees.

After working to control river blindness in some of the most endemic areas in Africa, in 1996 we assumed full responsibility for controlling the disease throughout Latin America, where the disease had been imported to six nations by African slaves. The affected communities were more scattered and the black flies had a shorter flight range. We decided to try two treatments annually, in the hope that we could reduce the microfilaria population enough to interrupt transmission, because the black flies would not find enough infection to carry the disease to the next humans bitten. This would require the treatment of at least 85 percent of infected persons in Brazil, Colombia, Ecuador, Guatemala, Mexico, and Venezuela. Within five

"I SOLD MY ROOF"

Ababora Abajobar does not regret selling his roof to feed his family. "The only hope I have is my children and my grandchildren, they are the only hope I have of the future," said Abajobar.
(EMILY STAUB)

The rolling, lush landscape of the Ethiopian countryside surrounded the straw and mortar shelter. Inside, Ababora Abajobar sat in the thick-walled darkness. Seventy years old, he kept his weathered hands on his walking stick, his blue socks neatly folded around his scarred shins.

As a young man, Abajobar recounted, he was strong and hardworking and his crop yields were bountiful. He had a wife and seven children. But over time, the living that sustained him also ruined him.

His coffee farm was situated alongside

a picturesque stream, making it an ideal setting to grow strong coffee plants, but the stream's current also created ideal conditions for black flies to breed. Biting flies are a daily nuisance for farmers working in the low-lying area, and Abajobar probably thought nothing of the swarming insects as he constantly waved them from his skin. It is estimated that he and his neighbors, men, women, and children, are bitten by these flies as many as twenty thousand times each year.

Today, the scars on his shins and his fading vision tell the story of what happened so long ago. Abajobar suffers from onchocerciasis, or river blindness, a parasitic disease spread by the bites of those irritating black flies. Approximately 17.7 million people worldwide are infected with the disease, and 123 million are at risk of it. The unbearable itching caused by the disease compelled Abajobar to scratch through layers of his skin, leaving pink trails of scars up and down his legs.

Hardship befell Abajobar when his wife died and he was afflicted with disease. The burden of caring for his children and farm by himself left him destitute.

"It's a terrible experience I have had. You can see my house here. I had a corrugated sheet metal cover, when I was desperately in need of money to feed my children. I just took off those sheets, and I sold my roof," Abajobar said.

In order to combat disabling illness caused by river blindness, The Carter Center, in partnership with Ethiopia's Ministry of Health and Lions Clubs International, developed a community-based health system to provide education to villages affected by the disease and to distribute Mectizan®, a drug donated by Merck & Co. This program has not only prevented millions of people from contracting river blindness but has also saved multitudes of communities from near extinction. People who once abandoned fertile land near rivers to avoid being bitten have returned to their land and revived their local economies.

Thanks to annual treatment with Mectizan®, Abajobar no longer suffers the effects of river blindness. The treatments will also ensure that future generations in the village will never suffer from the disease.

years, we found that five-year-old children in these villages did not harbor oncho microfilaria, although they were bitten as many as thirty thousand times a year. There is now no more blindness in Latin America from oncho, and we expect to reach our goal in 2011 of no further transmission of the disease. This achievement has convinced health authorities that it can be duplicated in some relatively isolated regions of Africa, and we have begun tests in Uganda and Sudan.

The Carter Center treats about 12 million people per year, with a cumulative total of 100 million treatments. In 1998, the program was expanded to include the prevention of lymphatic filariasis in African countries where the disease coexists with river blindness. An estimated 300 million Africans live in endemic communities, of whom about 40 million are infected by this disease. More than 50 million treatments of Mectizan® are now approved each year for lymphatic filariasis. This is a long-term commitment to donate as much of this medicine as necessary to treat both diseases, with the goal of eliminating them as public health problems.

LYMPHATIC FILARIASIS

The disease known as elephantiasis, or lymphatic filariasis (LF), causes grotesque swelling of the arms, legs, and sexual organs. More than 120 million people in the tropics are infected with LF, with at least 40 million disfigured or totally incapacitated.

This is a parasitic infection spread by mosquitoes, and it can be prevented and partially assuaged by a combined dose of two medicines, albendazole and Mectizan®, manufactured and distributed by GlaxoSmithKline and Merck. Their pledge of all the free doses necessary to deal with LF is the largest drug donation in history, valued at more than $1 billion. Our Center was persuaded to join a global program to eliminate LF because it fit so well into our ongoing efforts in several states where we were already working in Nigeria. Mectizan® was being used to combat river blindness, and we knew that bed nets and other control techniques for the LF mosquitoes would also kill those transmitting malaria.

In 2000, we began the program in Plateau and Nasarawa states, two of the most endemic in Nigeria. On our visits to affected areas, we have seen a wide range of cases. In a milder instance, the swelling of one young woman's right leg made it only about twice as large as the other, but it was covered by tiny parallel scars where her parents had made unsuccessful attempts to drain the excess fluid so she might have a chance to obtain a husband. Some of her more recent incisions were infected and were covered with a healing salve and light bandages provided by our Center. Her only other relief was to keep her leg elevated whenever possible. In some much worse cases, the infected arm or leg is almost the size of the stomach or chest.

One of our most disturbing encounters was with a row of men who were suffering from enlargement of their testicles. One of them seemed to have a basketball between his legs, and Dr. Frank Richards, director of our LF program, said that up to 30 percent of older men were infected in some villages. He added that the suicide rate was very high, and I could understand why.

We have delivered 16 million doses of the combination drugs that prevent LF, including 3.3 million in 2006, which covered more than 95 percent of the eligible population. The drugs also eliminate other intestinal worms, providing dramatic and long-lasting reductions in hookworm and roundworm infestations, thereby improving children's growth, mental ability, and nutrition. One promising factor is that a much higher global priority for combating malaria will assist in the control of lymphatic filariasis, since we and others have begun the delivery of

THE HOPE CLUB

Support groups help lymphatic filariasis victims like Hamisu Isa deal with the physical symptoms and social stigma of their affliction. (EMILY STAUB)

Sitting on a white plastic chair, Hamisu Isa, age thirty-five, listens to members of his lymphatic filariasis support group describe their symptoms, challenges, successes, and hopes. For years, he has suffered from the disease's severest form, elephantiasis.

Although Isa's leg and foot are enlarged and it was sometimes difficult for him to get around, he finds joy in little things that make his life easier. Today, he shows off a custom-made shoe. Typical flip-flops would not fit over his swollen foot, so a friend melted the strap off another shoe and attached it to a strap on Isa's shoe, creating a larger flip-flop and, as a result, a shoe that fits.

Isa is a member of The Hope Club, a support group in the central Nigerian city of Jos, where people suffering from lymphatic filariasis come together to discuss the physical challenges and social stigma of a disfiguring disease that causes grotesque swelling of arms, legs, and sexual organs. Because of their disability, victims cannot farm or carry out the basic daily tasks of living.

The Carter Center has assisted efforts to prevent lymphatic filariasis in Plateau and Nasarawa states in Nigeria, where an estimated 25 million people suffer from this disease, for which there is no cure. But it can be prevented through health education and annual single-dose combinations of oral medicines — albendazole, donated by GlaxoSmithKline, and Mectizan®, donated by Merck & Co. Because the disease is borne by mosquitoes, the same insecticide-treated bed nets that prevent the worldwide killer malaria can also prevent lymphatic filariasis.

"There is no cure, but there is hope," Carter Center expert John Umaru told the group. "If you keep your leg clean and treat cuts for infection, the swelling will not increase and may even decrease." The support group that Umaru leads is among the first of its kind. Participants learn about transmission and prevention of lymphatic filariasis and discuss techniques for preventing skin infections.

Isa said people would shun him, even his family, because the infection in his leg created a bad odor. With proper care, he stopped the running sores, and the swelling in his leg decreased.

"This shows other people that someday they can be better, too," said Umaru.

Given his challenges, Isa's story ends like a fairy tale. His skin looks clean, he sells T-shirts in the marketplace, he is getting his teaching certificate, and he is engaged to be married.

Perhaps someday there will be an epidemic of hope.

treated bed nets to kill the mosquitoes that transmit both LF and malaria. We received a promise from the president of Nigeria on this trip to furnish us nine million bed nets, and there is an even more ambitious and assured program under way in Ethiopia, as I'll describe later.

SCHISTOSOMIASIS

Schistosomiasis is another of the waterborne diseases now designated as neglected by the World Health Organization, which made it logical for us to adopt it as one of our Center's priorities in Africa. Relatively unknown in rich Western nations, the disease infects 200 million people in parts of Africa, South America, the Caribbean, a few countries in the Middle East, southern China, and Southeast Asia. It is the major health risk in rural areas of central China and Egypt, and it continues to rank high in other developing countries. In Egypt, schistosomiasis linked with cancer is the primary cause of death among men aged twenty to forty-five.

"Schisto," also known as snail fever or bilharzia, is another disease caused by parasitic worms. Freshwater becomes contaminated by *Schistosoma* eggs when infected people urinate or defecate in the water. The eggs hatch, and if certain types of snails are present in the water, the parasites grow and develop inside the snails. The microscopic parasites leave the snails and enter the water, and in a few seconds they can penetrate the skin of persons who are wading, swimming, bathing, or washing clothes. Within thirty to forty-five days, the parasites are transformed into male and female worms that live in blood vessels. The females lay from two hundred to two thousand eggs per day over an average of five years.

The adult worms are not detectable, but about half of their eggs travel through the body tissues to the bladder or intestines and cause pain when excreted, while the others attack the liver and other vital organs. Their damage is vividly indicated by blood in the urine or feces and by malnutrition as the worms compete with their host children for the food available in their limited diet. This disease is the second most common in Africa, behind malaria, and its numbers are rising as more ponds and dams are constructed for irrigation and other purposes. Not usually fatal, schisto is not given the same attention as HIV/AIDS, malaria, and tuberculosis.

In February 2007, Dr. Frank Richards led Rosalynn, John Hardman, Don Hopkins, and me to Nasarawa village, about a hundred miles from Abuja, the capital of Nigeria. We were greeted by government officials and more than ten thousand people, including what seemed to be all the school children in the area. In the front rows we saw large home-painted signs, welcoming us and espousing the battle against schistosomiasis. It was obvious from the texts that the causes of the disease and its treatment were well known. Along with the normal thanks to me and to The Carter Center, the children's messages were heartwarming: "I'm going to overcome schisto and become a teacher (doctor) (nurse) (president)."

We walked through the streets of the village until we reached the banks of the river Uke, in which several dozen children were swimming and women were washing clothes in the rocky places where the water was shallow. It was a beautiful scene, with the water clear and running smoothly. It was obvious that the river was the center of their lives. Someone brought me a plastic sandwich wrapper holding a half dozen black snails, each about the size of a small acorn. Dr. Richards, also in charge of the Center's schistomiasis program, repeated the description of the disease to the crowd packed closely around us. As leader of the Carter Center

315

team in the area, he had visited the village often, and told us quietly that 63 percent of the children were infected with schisto.

After our customary ceremonial speeches, Rosalynn and I moved to a central tent, where a line of children awaited us. We measured their heights and called out the number of praziquantel pills each should receive, beginning with one-half for the smallest and two for the largest. When we asked the children their ages, we found that the ten-year-olds were the size of a child about five years old who was not infected with intestinal worms.

We observed that an adult would receive three pills. As they swallowed their prescribed doses, Dr. Richards explained that this single dose of praziquantel, plus health education, is effective in containing the disease. The medicine reduces damage from the disease by up to 90 percent within six months of treatment, but it is almost always necessary to repeat the treatment. In communities where transmission is low, this interval may be up to five years.

Later we visited the health clinic, hidden among the slum dwellings, where groups of boys were lined up on wooden benches. I was pleasantly surprised at how knowledgeable they were about the disease within

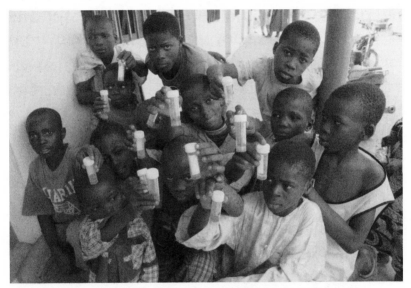

Boys hold vials containing urine samples bloodied by the schistosomiasis disease that they caught while swimming in the local river. (Louise Gubb)

their bodies. They knew that swimming in the river was the source of snail disease, but one boy said that the weather was very hot and they didn't have other water in which to swim or bathe. They often felt their skin itching when they emerged from the stream and believed that drying off would help. When I asked if it hurt to urinate, they all laughed and said, "Very much!" Prodded by a local nurse, they were eager to show me their urine, and each turned slightly away and then proudly exhibited his vial containing bloody urine.

With an annual grant of only forty thousand dollars, The Carter Center had been able to help treat 147,000 people in 2006, which brought our total to 943,000 during the seven years of our project. This is a small portion of known cases, so we have to rotate treatments, moving each year to the most severely endemic communities. Our greatest handicap is that the lowest price we have found (in South Korea) for each pill is seven cents, which is very near the cost of production. Unlike with the medicines or supplies we use for Guinea worm, trachoma, lymphatic filariasis, or onchocerciasis, no manufacturer or distributor had been willing to donate the drug until later in 2007, when a manufacturer announced a donation of 200 million tablets to the World Health Organization. Just $40 million would be required for enough praziquantel to treat the 200 million people in the whole world who now have the disease — plus, of course, the cost of delivering each dose and placing it in a patient's mouth.

I have visited the president of Nigeria twice to ask for enough money to help pay for pills and both times have been promised $2 million. Even in Africa's largest oil-producing country, these promises have not been honored.

When questioned, Dr. Richards said, "When you treat kids with praziquantel, they do better in their schoolwork, grow taller, and gain weight. They become more vigorous and active, like normal children. Unfortunately, these are forgotten diseases and forgotten people, and the pennies cannot be found."

TRACHOMA

Trachoma is the leading cause of preventable blindness in the world, but it is still known as one of the "neglected" diseases. It is caused by infection and can be treated, but 7 million people have been stricken blind by trachoma. An additional 500 million, usually the poorest and most forgotten in communities that are already struggling for survival, are at risk. In African countries, these are often areas where lymphatic filariasis, Guinea worm, schistosomiasis, and onchocerciasis are also endemic.

I knew about cases of trachoma as a boy, and I often had conjunctivitis, or sore eyes. As is the case now in our targeted areas of Africa, flies were everywhere, breeding in the excrement from both animals and humans. Our barn lot was nearby, and chickens, ducks, and geese ran freely in the yard. Screened doors and windows helped, but we also had to put a piece of gauze on top of any open pot or pitcher to keep the flies out of our milk or food. Fortunately, my mother was a nurse and a stickler for cleanliness, and our family had the only outdoor privy in the community. Trachoma was considered a threat to America in those early years, so doctors at Ellis Island used buttonhooks to examine the undersides of immigrants' eyelids and shipped those with trachoma back to their home countries.

Trachoma is caused by filthy and infected eyes, beginning as conjunctivitis and ultimately causing the upper eyelids to turn inward. Every blink drags the eyelashes across the corneas, causing pain like a thorn in the eye and then permanent blindness. The disease can be transmitted by contact with an infected person, by hands, a towel, or a garment, or carried by flies that have come in contact with discharge from infected eyes. Transmission is enhanced by an intimate relationship between mother and child or within a family or close-knit community.

Rosalynn and I had noticed during our visits to Masai and Dinka villages that, when seen from a distance, children appeared to be wearing eyeglasses, but when we approached them it was clear that rings of flies were sucking moisture from their eyes. The children rarely brushed the flies away and had never been taught to wash their faces.

In 1997, at the request of the Conrad N. Hilton Foundation, The Carter Center decided to make a major effort to help control trachoma in Ghana, Mali, Niger, and Nigeria, countries where the average annual income ranges from $100 to $370. We knew that trachoma only deepened the despair and poverty in these communities.

We began learning about the disease and raising funds to support the new program. Having been a district governor of Lions Clubs International during the mid-1960s, I knew that protecting eyesight was the organization's major benevolent project. I went to their Chicago headquarters to relay our plans, and they pledged a total of $16 million for five years, permitting an expansion of our program to Ethiopia and Sudan. The Hilton Foundation promised $13.6 million for a total of ten years.

The first cases of trachoma that we saw were in Mali, where Rosalynn, our Carter Center team, and I were joined by Jim Ervin, president of Lions Clubs International, and leaders of Lions Clubs in the country. Through an interpreter, we talked to a blind grandmother who said she was thirty years old. She was holding in her arms a little boy, about the same age as Amy's son, our youngest grandchild. Someone said, "The flies cluster shoulder to shoulder around an infected eye." With proper treatment, the grandson would never be blind.

Along with other organizations involved in the International Trachoma Initiative, we use the acronym SAFE as a guide to treatment: S = surgery, A = antibiotic, F = face cleaning, and E = environment.

Before surgery, victims carry crude tweezers, with which they pluck out all their eyelashes, but the hairs grow back even sharper. We are able to train nurses or physician's assistants to perform the simple surgery, a fifteen-minute procedure, to restore the eyelids to their normal position. On surgery

President Carter commended community members in Tingoli, Ghana, for their successful efforts to prevent the bacterial disease trachoma. (PETER DICAMPO)

day, hundreds of people desperate for relief stream into eyelid surgery camps run by the government and paid for by The Carter Center. We prefer a month of training, which costs six hundred dollars per worker, plus eight hundred dollars for two surgical instrument kits each. The materials for each operation cost about ten dollars.

In September 2000, Jim Ervin went with me to the headquarters of Pfizer Inc, the world's largest pharmaceutical company, where we met with corporate leaders and I spoke to several hundred of their assembled employees about trachoma. I described the SAFE program and emphasized that their antibiotic Zithromax® had proven to be most effective against the infection. I described how Merck had been contributing free Mectizan® for the treatment of onchocerciasis, and their CEO, William Steere, offered to provide Zithromax® whenever we could set up an effective system in a country for its use. Subsequently, Pfizer has expanded this commitment so that it now includes more than 135 million treatments. This is an invaluable contribution in fifteen of the fifty-five countries where trachoma is endemic.

Children can be taught by parents, teachers, or health workers to keep their faces clean, and the plethora of flies can be re-

In Amhara, Ethiopia, a young girl stands outside her household latrine. More than 350,000 latrines have been built in the region since 1997 to help prevent the spread of trachoma.
(EMILY STAUB)

duced by maintaining a sanitary environment using methods that are taken for granted in the developed world.

We combat trachoma in six countries, but our most intense effort is in the Amhara region of central Ethiopia, the most severely affected place in the nation. Our survey revealed that up to 80 percent of children there had early stages of the disease. Approximately 1.25 percent of all Ethiopians are blind, the highest incidence in the world, and more than 80 percent have some form of trachoma. Because mothers look after the children and children are the most heavily infected, women are three times more likely to develop the late stage of the disease. Usually the main workers in the house, women incapacitated with trachoma become a special burden. While their children may care for older blind women, younger women are frequently divorced by their husbands and sent back to their parents. In some communities in Ethiopia and Sudan, as many as 20 percent of women over fifteen years old are going blind and risk these social and economic punishments for their illness.

Dr. Paul Emerson joined The Carter Center as director for the Trachoma Control Program in November 2004. He had devoted nearly a decade to operational research and program evaluation in support of the global effort to control the disease, and under his leadership we quickly extended programs begun by Dr. Jim Zingeser to encourage face washing. Our latest reports from teachers and others show that more than 60 percent of the children are proudly demonstrating clean faces each morning.

The next stage of our program proved the most interesting and earned me a new reputation in Ethiopia. We learned that it was taboo for women to relieve themselves where they could be seen. They had to either defecate and urinate within their living compounds or restrain themselves until dark. One woman told Dr. Emerson, "I am a prisoner of daylight!" We decided to distribute simple plans for the construction of latrines: just dig a hole in the ground; fix the top with boards, stones, or concrete so it wouldn't cave in; and enclose it for privacy with brush, clay, or cloth. A latrine could be constructed for a cost of less than a dollar.

As latrines were being built and cleanliness became more important, many communities did not have access to enough soap, and they revived the lost craft of soap making. This provided not only an affordable method of sanitation but also a new product that women could sell to generate income.

We set an ambitious goal in Amhara district of ten thousand latrines during the first year, but we underestimated the power of women who saw them as a form of liberation. Family by family and village by village, latrine building was adopted as a major project, and 306,000 latrines were built within three years! We encouraged families to hang a gourd filled with water at each entrance, with a tiny hole at the bottom plugged with a stick. When we visited the area in 2005, people were especially proud to show us how they could now wash their faces and hands after using the privy. I became known as the Father of Latrines.

MALARIA

There is an apparent anomaly in the current statistics from the World Health Organization on annual deaths from diseases in the developing world, which seem to underestimate the ravages of malaria. In order of deadliness, (1) respiratory diseases come first at 4 million deaths per year, followed by (2) HIV/AIDS, 3 million, (3) malaria, 1 to 5 million, (4) diarrhea, 2.2 million, and (5) tuberculosis, 2 million. But the organization also states, "Malaria kills more than three thousand children each day in sub-Saharan Africa," which amounts to 1.1 million annu-

The four children of farmer Mamo Tesfaye sleep under long-lasting insecticidal bed nets to prevent bites from malaria-infected mosquitoes. (LOUISE GUBB)

ally just for this age group and geographic area. In Ethiopia, we know that annual deaths from HIV/AIDS are 130,000, while 270,000 die from malaria. This devastating disease causes a lifetime of suffering from chills, diarrhea, pain, and high fevers, with its fatalities concentrated among pregnant women and children in their first five years of life.

Malaria was prevalent in southwestern Georgia when I was growing up during the Great Depression, and it was not until 1946 that the Communicable Disease Center (CDC) was established, primarily to eliminate this disease. A year later, a vast effort was begun to screen houses and to spray outdoor wet places with DDT, and by 1950 only two thousand cases were reported. Malaria was considered eradicated from the United States by 1951. (The CDC subsequently became known as Centers for Disease Control and Prevention.) Meanwhile, the insecticide DDT has been banned from outdoor use in most nations since its devastating effect on wildlife became known.

Along with HIV/AIDS and tuberculosis, malaria qualifies as one of the "big three" diseases for which nations can qualify for financial grants from the Global Fund, a public-private partnership based in Switzerland. Nations that receive grants must quickly demonstrate that the money is being used wisely and effectively. In 2006, Ethiopian Prime Minister Meles Zenawi decided to make an all-out effort to reduce the threat of malaria throughout his nation, and we accepted his challenge to join in a partnership with the government ministries.

The plan was to utilize one of the most remarkable technological innovations of recent years — bed nets made of fibers that are impregnated before weaving with a pesticide whose lethal effect on mosquitoes would last for about seven years. Instead of merely being repelled by the nets, the insects would be killed on contact. There were 50 million people living in the endemic areas of Ethiopia, which meant that 20 million nets would be needed to provide an average of 2 per household. It would be a massive project to identify the communities to be included, acquire the nets, distribute them, and then ensure their proper installation, use, and care. The government would acquire 17 million nets using a portion of its Global Fund grant, its own resources, and support from other donors. We agreed to provide the remaining 3 million, be responsible for distributing bed nets in the areas where we already were controlling onchocerciasis and trachoma, and monitor the results for the seven-year period. As an added measure in certain areas, DDT would be used to spray interior walls of homes while being strictly prohibited from outdoor applications.

We located fourteen regional storage areas and began buying the bed nets before launching our six-month distribution effort in January 2007. It is hard to imagine the volume of 3 million nets. One enormous pile was named "Carter's Mountain." The total cost of our Center's portion of the malaria program in Ethiopia will be $46 million, an amount that we are attempting to raise from private contributors. This is the largest project in a single country that we have ever undertaken.

Advantages for our Center include a thorough knowledge of the malaria-endemic areas, derived from our battles against Guinea worm, trachoma, and onchocerciasis, along with a large cadre of trained native health workers who can now combine their efforts against several diseases simultaneously. As previously mentioned, the most direct ancillary benefit will be against lymphatic filariasis, since mosquitoes also spread this disease.

Task Force for Disease Eradication

The International Task Force for Disease Eradication (ITFDE) was formed at The Carter Center in 1988 to evaluate disease control and prevention and the potential for eradicating infectious diseases. Composed of scientists and notable international health organizations from around the world, the task force first met from 1988 to 1992, concluding that six diseases — dracunculiasis, poliomyelitis, mumps, rubella, lymphatic filariasis, and cysticercosis — could be eradicated. Some of these targets proved to be unrealistic, even if theoretically feasible. Guinea worm and polio eradication were already under way, but this ITFDE report has led to a new effort to eliminate lymphatic filariasis.

In June 2001, we were able to secure support from the Bill & Melinda Gates Foundation and resumed the effort to review progress in disease eradication and to make recommendations regarding opportunities for eradication or better control of certain diseases. Two diseases (Guinea worm and polio) have been designated by the World Health Organization for worldwide eradication, and five others (leprosy, lymphatic filariasis, river blindness, trachoma, and schistosomiasis) for elimination or dramatic reduction in specific regions. Not coincidentally, our Center's health programs address five of these seven diseases (all except polio and leprosy). In 2006, the ITFDE encouraged the Dominican Republic and Haiti to cooperate in eliminating malaria and lymphatic filariasis from the island of Hispaniola, and in 2007 it continued to monitor the potential for eliminating onchocerciasis in selected areas of Africa.

The task force also analyzes major diseases that become vulnerable to control thanks to new scientific knowledge or technological innovation. One notable example is the long-term impregnated bed nets for combating mosquito-borne malaria and lymphatic filariasis.

AGRICULTURE

Shortly after we left the White House, Rosalynn and I had a visit from Ryoichi Sasakawa, one of the most remarkable men we have known. Our first encounter with him was when his staff members called and requested permission to visit us at our home in Plains, along with Reverend Wayne Smith, founder of the Friendship Force. When the elderly Japanese man first entered our home, he expressed amazement that we lived in "such a humble dwelling." His second utterance was

334

"I understand that you need money to build a presidential library, and I want to make an initial contribution of $500,000."

This was obviously a favorable introduction, and we soon learned more about Mr. Sasakawa's background. He had been a famous fighter pilot in World War II, and at the war's end was imprisoned by General MacArthur for three years for alleged corruption and subversive activities involving Japan's military operations in the Orient. During this time of incarceration he devised an ingenious scheme for rejuvenating Japan's devastated industrial capability. When finally freed (without having been put on trial), Sasakawa developed a legal and official gambling syndicate. Since there were no lotteries, horse racing, or dog racing events, he built a network of lakes throughout Japan and designed standard speedboats on which bets could be placed.

The organization was first named the Japan Shipbuilding Industry Foundation, and several Japanese cabinet members, including the minister of transportation and finance, were designated to serve as directors. Gambling profits amounted to hundreds of millions of dollars, and practical control of these funds remained in Mr. Sasakawa's hands. When we first met him, he had established several

335

benevolent organizations around the world, one of which was the United States–Japan Foundation, which he endowed with $50 million. Sasakawa also made large contributions to UN agencies and expressed an interest in forming a partnership with The Carter Center to meet some benevolent needs in the developing world.

After several years of exploratory discussions, we decided to convene a meeting in Geneva with Sasakawa, the scientist Norman Borlaug, and me presiding. Our purpose was to find ways to increase the production of food grains in Africa, beginning with four nations as test cases. We selected Sudan, Ghana, Tanzania, and Zimbabwe so that we could employ the different seasons north and south of the equator. Sasakawa's foundation would provide the funding, I would represent The Carter Center in negotiating contracts with leaders of selected nations, and Borlaug would implement some of the agricultural techniques that had made him famous and earned him the Nobel Peace Prize in 1970 as the father of the Green Revolution in India and Pakistan. We decided that our project would be called Global 2000 (later changed to Sasakawa–Global 2000).

Along with our health programs, work with farm families in their fields gave us an unprecedented insight into their cultural practices. After our Global 2000 agriculture program had been implemented for a few years, we traveled to a few of the nations to honor the most outstanding farmers. One such visit was to a rural village in Zimbabwe about 125 miles from the capital city, Harare. I dressed that morning in the hotel as though I would be going to our own farm near Plains.

When we finally arrived at the site, we found several hundred villagers assembled in the village square, with young men and women already costumed and dancing. We were guided to two large trees, where a small man, proudly dressed in a wrinkled suit and tie, was standing under one of the trees and holding a plaque designating him as the outstanding farmer of the year. After exchanging ceremonial honors with the village chief and other dignitaries, we were invited to the farmer's home for lunch, served by his wife and daughters. When we finished eating, I suggested that we proceed to some of his fields to observe his agricultural management techniques. The vehemence of his objections was surprising, with an emphasis on the need to go through his animal pen, the heat of the midday sun, the likelihood of getting my clothes dirty, and the distance to the growing crops.

Pointing out that I was a farmer myself, accustomed to livestock manure and dressed in my work clothes, I finally prevailed, and our small entourage moved toward his cultivated fields, with his wife walking behind us with Rosalynn. On the way, the farmer and I exchanged comments about his cattle, and he was quite knowledgeable about this phase of his enterprise. Since our G2000 programs were restricted to food grains, I was eager to reach his field of maize (corn), whose quality had earned his honors. We could all see that it was an outstanding crop, approaching any yield that I might realize on our farm in Georgia.

Mostly as a courtesy, I asked a series of questions: "How wide do you space your rows?" "What variety of maize did you choose?" "When did you apply the fertilizer, and what formula was used?" "Did you have any problem with insects?"

It quickly became obvious that our host knew nothing about the crop. Finally, he just turned to his wife, who provided all the answers. She was obviously the only farmer in the family, and she and the children had made all the decisions and done all the work, while her husband took care of the cattle — and the money when the crop was sold.

Women in Ghana sort a variety of corn called quality protein maize. Children weaned on quality protein maize are larger and healthier than those weaned on normal corn. (ANNEMARIE POYO)

The Carter Center has a special relationship with Ethiopia. My first contact was with the Communist dictator Mengistu Haile Mariam, who was infamous for having smothered Haile Selassie in August 1975 during a coup that ended the emperor's reign of almost forty years. Mengistu established a Marxist regime known as the Derg, closely affiliated with the Soviet Union and anathema among the democracies of the Western world.

I had just descended from the peak of Mount Kilimanjaro in August 1988 on a climb with Rosalynn, two of our sons, and three grandchildren when we received a message through the government of Tanzania asking if we would make a side trip to Ethiopia before returning home. Representatives of the International Red Cross and the UN High Commissioner for Refugees were being obstructed by the Derg leader from delivering food, water, and medicine to two refugee camps. One was in the north, for Somalians, and the other in the southwest, for Sudanese, all of whom were escaping the warfare in their countries. Although the United States had strained diplomatic relations with Ethiopia and we had no ambassador there, I agreed to attempt a resolution. We requested a meeting with Mengistu through his embassy in Dar es Salaam and then immediately flew to Addis Ababa.

When we arrived at our hotel, an aide of Mengistu was waiting with an invitation to visit him as soon as we were acclimated to the altitude of a mile and a half. It seemed likely to us that he was eager to have any possible contact with a respected leader from the West. I wanted to learn more about the refugee problem and to draft my best proposal for its solution, so we decided to postpone our visit until nine o'clock the next morning.

The Ethiopian leader welcomed Rosalynn and me, and we spent about twenty minutes exchanging pleasantries. I noticed that he had an interpreter but would often respond to my comments or questions without waiting for the translation. As soon as possible, I reviewed the facts about the apparent impasse, with which he agreed, and then I proposed that his troops escort the relief agency personnel and supervise their work, but without interfering with the delivery of necessary supplies to the refugees. He paused for just a few seconds and then responded, "Good. I accept this proposal."

When we stood and prepared to leave, he asked if I would grant him a request. I said,

"Yes," and he asked that we dine with him that night in his private quarters. I talked to several foreign diplomats during the afternoon, learning all I could about the sustained bombing and strafing of Eritrea by the Ethiopian air force. The revolutionary war had begun as soon as Mengistu took power, and the fighting had intensified. I hoped to help reduce the bloodshed.

Rosalynn and I arrived for dinner at the beginning of a torrential downpour, and we were met by a servant and ushered into something like an enclosed sunporch, with a somewhat flat double roof covered by corrugated metal. Although the noise of the rain was quite loud, it was obviously too late to move the elaborate meal preparations. Mengistu joined us and was soon followed by his wife. We agreed later that she was one of the most beautiful women we had ever met, with the aura of one of King Solomon's princesses. We had a pleasant conversation, during which I explored the possibility of peace talks between Ethiopia and Eritrea. Mengistu authorized me to contact the leaders of the revolutionary Eritreans, and later The Carter Center conducted discussions for a total of twenty-eight days, divided between Atlanta and Nairobi. Although we never concluded a final peace agreement, the level of combat was drastically reduced.

At least indirectly, these negotiations led to my subsequent acquaintance with a Tigrayan guerrilla fighter named Meles Zenawi. During one of our visits to Sudan, where we had a Global 2000 agricultural project to increase the production of wheat, I was asked to meet with Meles and told that the only suitable venue would be the airport. He quickly informed me that, as leader of the Tigrayan People's Liberation Front (TPLF), he was determined to overthrow Mengistu's regime and had an alliance with a group from Eritrea with the same goal. Meles was a small man, quiet and personally modest, but he spoke with total authority and confidence. He unrolled a map of northern Ethiopia and showed me where his and Mengistu's troops were located and the Tigrayans' planned route to Addis.

I met with Meles on two other occasions during my frequent trips to Africa — always at airports, where we examined his maps together on a table or the floor. He didn't seem to be in a special hurry but emphasized to me the inexorability of his campaign. His troops would move southward perhaps ten miles at a time, then pause to solidify their good relations with the local populace. They would purchase grain to feed the TPLF troops and make sure that the occupied communities were not harmed before making further military advances. On one occasion, Meles showed me where twenty Derg tanks were located south of a small river and marshaled for a counterattack against his troops. There was a bridge across the stream, and I asked Meles why he didn't blow it up to deter the prospective attack. He smiled and responded that he didn't want to destroy the nation his people would soon be governing.

The combined forces of the Tigrayans and Eritreans reached Addis Ababa in May 1991, and Mengistu and his family fled to Zimbabwe, where they still reside. Meles Zenawi became president of the transitional government and soon asked The Carter Center to assist in its early stages of development. There has always been an absolutely firm requirement that Ethiopians make their own decisions, but we have given requested advice and support in drafting a constitution, establishing a judiciary system that could deal with the multiple war crimes of the Derg, providing human rights training to police officers, and assisting in programs involving agriculture, education, and health. The new leaders adopted a parliamentary system of government, and Meles became the prime minister.

After we had established our Global 2000 agriculture program in a few other countries, Prime Minister Meles Zenawi requested that we help his farmers increase their production of wheat and maize. We got off to a good start in 1993 with just 161 farmers, and the following year we had 1,600 in our program. Rosalynn and I went to Ethiopia to inspect the project and to make an award to the outstanding farmer.

Meles accepted our invitation to go about 60 miles north of Addis to visit three farms producing wheat on vertisol land. This is thick clay that changes from sticky gumbo mud to cracked dry surfaces with practically no percolation of moisture. The average yield of wheat using traditional practices here is only half a ton per hectare. Our G2000 farmers were producing from four to five tons, planted on an elevated seedbed about three feet wide with a deep furrow around and using a modest application of fertilizer. This was the most dramatic result I had seen in Africa, and Meles was overwhelmed. Farmers were either delighted or unbelieving, the latter looking at the developing grain heads and saying, "We'll have to wait and count the bags." So far, our agricultural specialist, Dr. Marco Quiñones, had trained five hundred extension workers, with one deployed in each village.

We gave the award to a small woman and her two daughters, then drove to Addis. During the return trip, Meles was very aggressive in urging me to expand our Global 2000 program.

"How many Ethiopian farmers could you include next year?"

"We hope to go from sixteen hundred to sixteen thousand, and then level off at about forty thousand."

His next question caused me to stop our vehicle. "Is it possible to have four hundred thousand?"

I invited Dr. Quiñones to join us, and he explained to Meles that in Ghana we had included too many farmers and failed to accommodate the enormous quantity of maize produced. Proper storage was inadequate, and the market crashed as excess grain flooded it. By the time we reached our hotel, a tentative agreement had been reached. We would adhere to our established limit but would assist the Ethiopian government in adding a large number of additional farmers who could copy our program. This was done during the next two years, and Ethiopia was able to export grain for the first time in modern history. Because of the lack of an adequate transportation system, the problem of transferring surplus grain from one part of the nation to another still remains.

One of the challenges that Meles Zenawi inherited was an absence of higher education, especially in health care. In a conversation with Rosalynn, John Hardman, and me, he suggested that we might help to overcome this problem. What we called the Ethiopia Public Health Training Initiative (EPHTI) was launched in 1997 to improve the health of Ethiopians by enhancing the training of health personnel.

Our collaborative program involving the ministries of health and education has created opportunities for Ethiopian teachers and professors to work side by side with international experts in developing curricula and learning materials based on local community needs and experience. Teachers at seven Ethiopian universities use these materials to train health specialists, who, in turn, train and manage community health workers.

The universities that are part of EPHTI hold workshops to draft and produce training materials such as modules and lecture notes on chronic and life-threatening diseases, longer-term health promotion, and disease-prevention activities. Topics have included health care principles, individual tropical diseases, nutrition, maternal and child health, mental health, reproductive health, water and sanitation, risk behavior modification, and others. For each of the universities we have been able to provide U.S. $15,000 worth of textbooks and reference books, computers, printers, photocopiers, at least a dozen periodical and journal subscriptions, and basic laboratory equipment, such as anatomical models and microscopes.

In February 2007 we invited nine other African nations to send their ministers of education and health to Addis Ababa, where we had a "replication" conference to induce them to learn what might be done in their own countries. By that time, we had furnished $8.7 million and helped our Ethiopian partners develop training texts for 65 known diseases and health challenges, 101 lecture booklets, and 538 regional workshops; train more than 700 faculty and 17,400 health extension workers; and graduate 7,135 students from the seven regional universities. During the next two years we will bring the total number of health workers to 30,000 (one for every 2,500 people), plus 5,000 health officers with training equivalent to that of registered nurses or physician's assistants.

Our next challenge will be to spread these benefits to as many other nations as possible.

CHAPTER FIVE
BUILDING HOPE

HUMAN RIGHTS

The overall umbrella under which all Carter Center projects can be covered is "human rights." Most Americans, not excluding me when I was in public office, would assume that these basic rights encompass freedom of speech, religion, assembly, trial by jury, and the right to choose our own leaders. Although these political rights are important to everyone, we have seen that they fade into secondary importance when a family does not have food, shelter, clothing, or any prospect for education, medical care, or peaceful existence. The easy resolution of this apparent dilemma is for "human rights" to include people's needs for political, social, and economic rights.

Because I had declared while I was president that human rights would be the foundation for our nation's foreign policy, it was inevitable that our Center would adopt the

Jimmy and Rosalynn Carter assess Carter Center fieldwork in Ethiopia in 2005. (Vanessa Vick)

same priority. We first decided to address the political issues, realizing that there were several dozen nongovernmental organizations dedicated to various aspects of these rights. They concentrated on geographic regions, the torture or mistreatment of prisoners, or the abuse of journalists, doctors, or members of other professions. The pre-eminent groups needed to coordinate their efforts to ensure that no aspect of human rights abuse was overlooked. We also made an effort to preempt or avoid abuses, rather than just react after they had occurred. We recognized that the most terrible human rights crimes were perpetrated during civil war or by despotic leaders against an entire people. The other generic problem was that there was no internationally accepted leader or organization that could speak or act for the global community.

We brought together at The Carter Center about two dozen representatives of key organizations, including Amnesty International, Americas Watch, Helsinki Watch, the Inter-American Court of Human Rights, the Lawyers Committee for Human Rights, the International League of Human Rights, the Palestinian Independent Commission for Citizens' Rights, the Jacob Blaustein Institute for the Advancement of Human

Rights, and scholars and noted activists who were devoted to defending human rights. In our discussions, it became clear that there needed to be more publicity about violations of rights and about what could be done to address this serious problem.

During all the years since I left the White House, I have routinely considered individual cases of human rights violations. Each of the hundreds of cases is first assessed for authenticity and substance by our human rights director, Karin Ryan, and our Center staff, then legally by volunteers from the Emory law school. I then decide how best to intercede, usually with a private letter or telephone call directly to the head of state involved. We point out that a violation has been reported, that it is contrary to the basic laws of the nation, and that the global human rights community is deeply concerned. We include enough specific facts to make it clear that we are thoroughly familiar with the case. We outline possible actions that could prevent public condemnation being focused on the abuse, and I request a response that can clarify the situation.

The best option is for corrective action to be taken by the perpetrators of the mistreatment, which allows them to take credit for progress and establish better procedural policy for the future. We have achieved positive results in a surprising number of cases but sometimes receive only a long legal justification for an imprisonment or punishment and at other times get no response at all. We are inclined to be persistent and join other human rights organizations in a public condemnation when this seems to be the only remaining approach.

One of the greatest unmet needs in many nations was the recognition and protection of human rights heroes. Almost invariably, their personal courage is directly proportional to the level of abuse perpetrated by their rulers. We found a kindred soul in Mrs. Dominique de Menil, an American heiress best known for her devotion to the arts. She offered to furnish an annual human rights prize of $100,000 if we would join in the selection of recipients and in presentation of the prizes. We established the Carter-Menil Human Rights Foundation in 1986 to support our Center's efforts and to award an annual prize. These highly publicized ceremonies became a major factor in promoting the concept of human rights.

The awards ceremonies were usually conducted at our Center, at Mrs. De Menil's Rothko Chapel in Houston, Texas, or in New York, and scheduled during the second week in December to correspond with the anniversary of the Universal Declaration of Human Rights. With the help of many people, I prepared and delivered a series of annual human rights addresses, each designed to emphasize a different aspect of the subject.

Our prize recipients were chosen from different areas of the world to represent the most disturbing examples of oppression. Our first honorees were Yuri Orlov, Soviet physicist and dissident, and the Group for Mutual Support (GAM), an organization of families of disappeared persons in Guatemala. During subsequent years our panel chose the Vicaría de la Solidaridad, a Chilean group that provided legal aid to political prisoners and assistance to the families of victims of human rights abuse; the Sisulu family of South Africa, whose courage symbolized the fight against apartheid; Al-Haq and B'Tselem, organizations that represented the Arab and Jewish communities in the Middle East and were striving to publicize and reduce persecution of people in the occupied Palestinian territories; and the Consejo de Comunidades Etnicas "Runujel Junam" (CERJ) in El Salvador. Six of its members had been murdered and one disappeared during the year because of their public condemnation of government oppression.

One year we departed from our previous policy to give a posthumous award, to the Human Rights Institute of the University of Central America on behalf of six Jesuit priests slain in El Salvador. This was our largest ceremony, attended by Nelson Mandela and honoring fifteen Latin American human rights activists. Another annual prize was divided between two organizations in the United States that protected the rights of Native Americans and refugees: the Native American Rights Fund and the Haitian Refugee Center. We had a special ceremony in 1994 to honor Norwegians for the accords they negotiated that gave Palestinians some political rights and promised progress toward peace. The PLO chairman, Yasir Arafat, Israeli foreign minister Shimon Peres, and Queen Sonja of Norway joined us as we presented our monetary prize to the Institute of Applied Social Science for taking the lead in the mediation effort. In addition, we dedicated a large Anthony Smith sculpture, *Marriage,* to the people of Norway.

The many successes of the United Nations are sometimes buried in the criticisms of those who do not acknowledge the organization's value. The human rights bodies of the UN are especially controversial because they often fall victim to the paralysis of intergovernmental politics. It is important to remember that the UN is governed by almost two hundred nations that are constantly vying for influence or pushing back against laws or regulations with which they have disagreements. It is remarkable when anything is achieved under these circumstances, but the UN can boast of many great accomplishments, and it enjoys considerable legitimacy in most of the world.

It became evident after the end of the Cold War that global cooperation on the advancement of human rights and democracy would have to replace the post–World War II paradigm, with the West battling with Communism over which system would prevail. In addition to awarding the Carter-Menil prizes, The Carter Center assumed a major role in pressing for a human rights system within the United Nations that could be a forum for victims of oppression and also help to induce abusive governments to remedy their policies.

We adopted two major projects to provide more international cooperation in countering and preventing human rights crimes. Since the UN Human Rights Commission in Geneva had become relatively ineffective because its membership was packed by oppressive regimes that wanted to protect themselves from criticism, we decided to promote the creation of a UN high commissioner for human rights, whose work would parallel that of the existing commissioner for refugees. I first broached this idea publicly at a UN conference on human rights in Vienna in 1993, but we found that UN Secretary-General Boutros Boutros-Ghali was adamantly opposed, claiming that it would be an additional bureaucracy and that he was, in effect, already performing this important function.

The Carter Center and other organizations mounted a major effort, and four years later the office was established, with the high commissioner given preeminent responsibility for enhancing human rights by promoting international cooperation, stimulating and coordinating action, raising standards, preventing violations, responding to abuses, assisting official and nonofficial organizations, and providing education and publicity.

The genocide in Rwanda in 1994 precipitated our interest in joining African leaders from the region in overcoming the aftermath of the mass assassinations, promoting harmony within the Great Lakes region, and helping to prevent similar atrocities. It became increasingly obvious that there was no international organization designed to punish the perpetrators or to deter others. Ad hoc systems of justice had to be created after each case, a process that required many years and resulted in frustration and uncertainty. We decided to join in a global effort, led by numerous human rights organizations and begun by the prime minister of Trinidad and Tobago, to create a permanent International Criminal Court (ICC). Its judicial procedures and staffing would be continuous, and serious generic crimes — including "war crimes," "crimes against humanity," and "genocide" — would be addressed.

We convened early planning sessions at our Center, and Karin Ryan, our human rights director, monitored the progress of the ICC proposal through a long and hotly contested process. In July 1998 the statute of the ICC was adopted by 120 nations, with seven (Iraq, Israel, Libya, China, Qatar, the United States, and Yemen) in opposition. President Bill Clinton reversed his position in December 2000 and signed the treaty, which obliged the United States to refrain from acts that would defeat its object and purpose, but the United States and Israel "unsigned" the treaty in 2002 in order to avoid these obligations.

Despite this opposition, sixty-six states had ratified the ICC by July 2002, authorizing it to prosecute crimes committed after this date. One of the restraints is that the court can exercise its jurisdiction only when national courts are unwilling or unable to investigate or prosecute the specified crimes. The court consists of eighteen judges, elected for up to nine years, and a prosecutor has the responsibility to act when authorized. Investigations have been initiated into three situations — Uganda, Democratic Republic of Congo, and Darfur. The court issued its first arrest warrants in 2005. The first pre-trial hearings were held in 2006.

Support for the ICC has continued to grow. As of 2007, 145 nations had signed the statute and 104 of them had ratified it, but a number of states, including the United States, Israel, and China, continue their opposition. Despite polls showing that 69 percent of Americans support U.S. participation in the ICC, the United States attempts to force signatory nations to sign agreements exempting Americans and has cut aid to many countries that refuse to yield to this pressure. Recently, the United States has agreed to cooperate with the ICC when it is acting against our "enemies," as defined by the White House. There is little doubt that oppressive dictators will be restrained in committing terrible crimes by the existence of the ICC and the demonstrated aggressiveness of the prosecutor.

The Carter Center's Human Rights Program has worked from the perspective that people can transform their own societies into democracies with respect for human rights without outside interference, as long as governments do not repress those who are trying to implement reforms. Increasingly, we have had to examine the impact of the fundamental shift in U.S. policy in recent years that has wide implications for the entire concept of human rights — that every individual has unalienable rights. This concept, which gave birth to our nation and has inspired freedom lovers everywhere, was suddenly being eroded in more substantial ways than at any time in recent history.

Since 2001, the U.S. government has abandoned its role as a champion of human rights and has perpetrated terrible and illegal abuses in prisons in Abu Ghraib and Guantánamo, sent prisoners secretly to other nations to be tortured, denied the applicability of Geneva Convention restraints, and severely restricted time-honored civil liberties within our own country. Certain political leaders of other nations, who are inclined to perpetrate human rights abuses to quiet dissenting voices and were previously restrained by positive influence from Washington, now feel free to emulate or exceed the abuses approved by American leaders.

In November 2003, not long after the Iraq War began, The Carter Center convened our first human rights defenders conference. The activists who attended were reeling from the consequences of abusive U.S. policies. At our conference, we heard devastating stories from participants from forty-one countries. We learned that lawyers were being accused of abetting terrorism in Nepal and Tunisia simply for doing their jobs; Egypt felt emboldened by the U.S. example to ignore international concern for detaining and torturing critics of government policy; and activists in India were alleged to be terrorists simply for distributing a pamphlet about the rights of detainees. These participants said that all the gains they had made to advance human rights through decades of sacrifice and risk were being lost as governments renewed their authoritarian tenden-

The Carter Center's Human Rights Defenders Forum brings together activists worldwide to spotlight threats to civil liberties and strengthen protections for human rights. (ANNEMARIE POYO)

(DEBORAH HAKES)

cies, assuming they would no longer have to bow to international pressure about human rights violations.

To address this continuing challenge, The Carter Center now convenes an annual meeting designed to protect and strengthen the effectiveness of human rights defenders. My co-chair is always the UN high commissioner for human rights, and we include the key organizations that are active on an international scale. Our honored guests and prime participants are the heroes who have suffered from oppressive regimes, along with activists who represent the United Nations as official rapporteurs with the responsibility of investigating and reporting on the most serious abuses. Although some of the defenders are in prison or otherwise prevented from coming to Atlanta, we attempt to give maximum publicity to their plight. I usually write an editorial for publication in major news media to summarize the findings of our convocations.

One of the human rights defenders' reports was a major factor in my writing *Palestine Peace Not Apartheid.* Mustafa Barghouti, a Palestinian doctor active in an independent political party that seeks a nonviolent resolution to the Israeli-Palestinian conflict, talked to us about the village of Qalqilya in the West Bank. He said:

Imagine a city where 46,000 people are surrounded by a wall from all directions with one little entrance, a gate. The gate has a key, and Israeli soldiers keep the key. They shut off the city every day at 6:00 p.m. and open it the next morning. Sometimes they decide not to open the gate at all for several days. During the last month, before I came here, the city was entirely shut off for ten days. The people in Qalqilya called me and said, "We don't even see the sunset anymore because the wall that surrounds us is eight to twelve meters high."

I am also a medical doctor. I do not think it is a coincidence that you have so many medical doctors participating in human rights activities. There is nothing as drastic and as sad as struggling to have a pregnant woman ready to give birth trying to cross a checkpoint to receive medical care. Fifty-three women so far have been obliged to give birth at checkpoints. The last woman who gave birth in this way, in Jenin, was standing twenty meters from an ambulance and the Israeli guards wouldn't let her across to get to it. We have lost eighty-nine people already who were having heart attacks or children who were having respiratory problems who were not allowed to cross to receive medical care.

It is a small country, the West Bank and Gaza, but in this little tiny place you have 482 checkpoints that have prevented freedom of movement for the last two and a half years. How many other times in history has a whole population been prevented from using roads and streets — their own roads and streets — for month after month? A trip that would usually take forty-five minutes from Ramallah to the Hebron area would now take, if it were possible at all, nine hours after changing vehicles at least eleven times. This is so drastic and so terrible and so unacceptable that something must be done about it.

We feel a responsibility to communicate these kinds of messages to the American people and to the international community. In addition to my own writing, we provide a global forum for these defenders to describe their problems in an annual roundtable discussion telecast by media such as CNN International, and we then take a representative group to Washington to meet with key members of Congress and the administration. Defenders from Egypt, Palestine,

Zimbabwe, Liberia, Kenya, Colombia, and other nations appeal to American leaders to reassert our nation's commitment to the honoring of international human rights laws and to use our influence to prevent abuses in other countries.

In a meeting with Paul Wolfowitz, then deputy secretary of defense, Saad Eddin Ibrahim, an Egyptian professor, reported having served part of a seven-year sentence of hard labor for publishing a criticism of Egyptian elections. Wolfowitz had pushed for the United States to exert pressure on the Egyptian government to release Ibrahim, but he was visibly upset by Ibrahim's claim that U.S. policy was undermining human rights and democracy movements. He was preparing to leave the meeting in anger when Dr. Willy Mutunga, a Kenyan human rights defender who had also paid the price of prison time in his quest for democracy, spoke about the direct impact of U.S. policy in his own country.

Mutunga explained that the U.S. ambassador to Nairobi had been pressing the newly elected Kenyan government to pass the Suppression of Terrorism Bill, a bill that rights groups feared would reverse recent democratic achievements there. Two weeks later, the ambassador invited Mutunga to meet him and initiated a dialogue about the proposed law. Apparently the United States dropped its support, and the bill remains in limbo.

In the summer of 2005, Senator John McCain met with a group of human rights defenders after our annual conference. They made the case to him and other leaders that American policies were making their jobs harder because repressive governments point to U.S. actions related to torture and detention. Karin Ryan and others worked with Senator McCain over the next few months as he introduced legislation to ban torture. This was an important first step in forcing the U.S. Congress to correct abusive policies and practices of the executive branch of government.

EQUALITY FOR WOMEN

One of the problems that became increasingly obvious to us was the almost universal discrimination against women, not only in America but throughout the world. The foundation for this unequal treatment is within the major religions, which are almost impervious either to criticism or to change. Discrimination against women is overt and official in many Arab nations, where women must remain veiled, cannot operate automobiles or compete with men for a job, and often receive inferior if any education. Women are prohibited from serving as priests in Roman Catholic and most Orthodox churches, and some Protestant denominations are even more discriminatory. Quoting some selective Bible verses, the Southern Baptist Convention mandates that wives must be "submissive" to their husbands; that women cannot serve as military chaplains, pastors, or even deacons; and that it is improper for women to instruct men.

In many parts of Africa, our Center's health and agriculture programs have provided us with unprecedented opportunities for observation of societal habits. In most rural societies, women are required to do the majority of the manual labor while men treat them as chattel and control family financial affairs. Mandatory female circumcisions are still pervasive as religious rites, and it is taboo for any woman to urinate or defecate where she might be seen, even though no private places for women to relieve themselves exist.

In order to draw attention to this issue in our own country, we decided to conduct a major conference to promote sexual equality, choosing the observance of the bicentennial of the U.S. Constitution as an appropriate date. We planned a large assembly of historians, political and social scientists, statisticians, religious leaders, and specialists in human rights, labor, education, and other relevant subjects.

Our original framework literally exploded, as women from all over America responded. The official sponsors were Rosalynn and First Ladies Betty Ford, Lady Bird Johnson, and Pat Nixon. Fifteen hundred delegates from all fifty states and ten foreign countries came to listen closely to 150 speakers and panelists. Among the notable leaders were the civil rights heroines Rosa Parks, Delores Tucker, Coretta Scott King, Eleanor Holmes Norton, Leola Brown Montgomery (mother of the plaintiff in *Brown v. Board of Education*), and Representative Barbara Jordan of Texas; the champions of women's rights Sarah Weddington from Texas and Eleanor Smeal; Supreme Court Justice Sandra Day O'Connor and future justice Ruth Bader Ginsburg; and the political leaders Jane Harman, Olympia Snowe, and Geraldine Ferraro. The discussions covered the heroic but largely ignored role of women in the founding of our nation despite an absence of civil or legal rights, still existing differences in opportunities, and specific recommendations.

Written and video curricula were developed and distributed for classes at the high school and university levels, and the conference proceedings were contributed to the National Archives and major libraries for future study and scholarly research. Since then, we have made a special effort to exalt the status of women in all the Center's programs, to emphasize in our published reports the key role they already play in promoting health, agriculture, and political reforms, and to expand their participation in the future.

The Carter Center remained involved in efforts to raise awareness of the rights of women on an international level, and was represented at the Beijing World Conference on Women in 1995, emphasizing efforts to treat violence against women as a violation of human rights. This was a needed effort because women are often left behind by traditional human rights campaigns. Private individuals are responsible for most incidents of violence against women, yet some suggest that human rights violations can be committed only by governments, given their unique position to accept and honor human rights treaties. Women's rights advocates successfully challenged this idea in Beijing and afterward, when violence against women was fully integrated into the crimes covered by the Rome Statute of the International Criminal Court. These gains mean that governments that do not take action to protect women against acts of violence, even private acts, could be considered in violation of their human rights obligations.

In 2000, Karin Ryan helped to ensure that, for the first time, language was introduced to condemn so-called honor killings as a violation of fundamental human rights. The language was vociferously opposed by some governments of Islamic nations on the grounds that it singled out Muslim societies when violence against women is a worldwide phenomenon. A compromise was finally accepted, to include the term "crimes of passion" alongside "honor killings."

I am returning home from Nepal as I write this, having observed the parliament decide that 50 percent of all constitutional assembly delegates chosen by political parties will have to be women. This is a notable example of progress being made.

THE ATLANTA PROJECT

During our first decade, Carter Center projects were focused on problems in foreign countries, and I always gave a thorough report on my trips abroad to Emory University's president, Jim Laney. After one of our regular visits to several African nations, Jim asked, "Have you ever considered taking care of some of the problems here at home?"

He and I decided that The Carter Center would embark on an analysis of the most crucial needs among poor people in the Atlanta area to see if there was a legitimate role for us. One of the things I requested was an opportunity to examine the census data so that I could understand in which areas we could detect the most significant differences among people. After viewing slides for an hour or so, I finally asked for two of them to be projected on the screen simultaneously: the percentage of homes with a single parent (invariably a woman) and the residences of babies born to teenage girls. A broad and clear band extended across the southern part of the city, encompassing portions of three counties. We then found consistent correlations with indicators related to educational level, income, and unemployment.

We assessed this information further and decided to announce an effort to assist people in the designated areas in raising their standard of living. At a meeting with Atlanta business and professional leaders, I made a public commitment to assume this responsibility, and the civic leaders pledged their

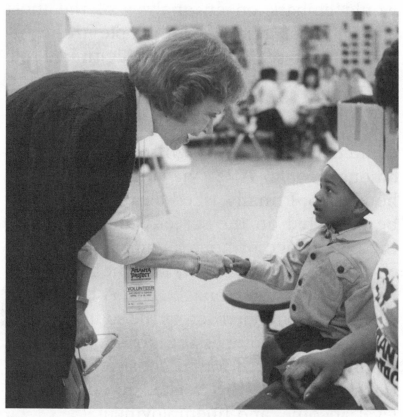

Rosalynn Carter greets a small child and his mother during a community visit as part of The Atlanta Project. (THE CARTER CENTER)

support. I proposed the name The Atlanta Project, which was soon shortened to TAP. I asked forty influential citizens to help by raising funds, at least $5 million annually, and everyone accepted my request.

We came to realize that the designated area encompassed 500,000 people. After dividing the area into twenty parts, called "cluster communities," each including about 25,000 people, we began learning as much as possible about them. I had been lecturing for at least six hours each month at Emory, and Jim Laney and I decided that, for a time, I would move a portion of this time to my work at The Carter Center in order to concentrate on TAP.

Although Atlanta has a justifiable reputation for good race relations — and is known as "the city too busy to hate" — we found a startling and sharp divide between "haves" and "have-nots," regardless of race. An elite group of black political leaders had governed the city since 1974, working closely with whites who dominated business and professional affairs. The citizens of the TAP communities were predominantly African Americans — many of them poor, isolated, and largely neglected. We found that the professionals in welfare, health, education, police protection, and even sanitation tended to live in more affluent communities and commuted each day to work in our targeted areas. The social disconnect between public employees and the families they served was almost complete.

Corporations advertised employment opportunities in the local newspapers, which had minimal circulation in the TAP area, so people who needed jobs would never know that Delta Air Lines desired flight attendants, or that there were job openings in other corporations. Checks to welfare recipients were usually cashed by local moneylenders, who charged a standard fee of eight dollars or more per check, or by owners of small stores, who charged very high prices for merchandise. Government agencies, such as the federal department of Housing and Urban Development, would not accept an endorsed welfare check for payment. An analysis by Georgia State University revealed that an average of sixty-four pages of government forms was required to obtain final approval of a poor family's application for housing, welfare, food stamps, Medicaid, or enrollment of children in a Head Start program.

Rosalynn made a test shopping trip to grocery stores and found that the same cans of soup were being sold for $1.40, often on credit, that she bought at uptown super-markets for a third as much. Banks were reluctant or unwilling to permit residents of the large government housing units to open checking accounts. House-to-house surveys revealed that few children were immunized, police surveillance was often sporadic or consisted of police merely driving through a housing project in a patrol car with the windows rolled up, and drug dealers preyed on vulnerable families to secure operating bases in private homes. Any homeowner who reported this harassment was required to make a formal complaint and promise to testify, before the police would take protective action. This action almost invariably brought punishment or threats from the criminals. Although there were a number of local leaders, they usually "governed" their communities autocratically, based on self-anointed positions derived from their ambition, charisma, shrewdness, or dominant personalities. Few citizens had any role in voicing requests or complaints or any means of contacting the "outside world."

I had been governor and president of these same people and had never been aware of their plight except on a general basis derived from statistics and a few individual crises that were publicized. Now, what could we do?

President Carter signs up children in Atlanta neighborhoods for immunization shots during The Atlanta Project. (MICHAEL SCHWARZ)

We began by establishing a small secretariat and an advisory committee as broadly representative as possible, whose members met with me regularly. I assigned a cluster community to each adviser and required a monthly status report. We decided that every cluster should have a coordinator and an assistant, both of whom had to meet high professional standards and reside permanently in the area. Recognizing the need for both jobs and the capability of relating to government and private agencies, we decided to ask each of the top twenty corporations in Atlanta to form a partnership (not sponsorship) with one cluster community. They were required to assign a vice president or other top manager to work full-time on this project, to immerse themselves in their area, and to help form local committees on key subjects, teach residents how to prepare and submit grant requests, and recruit hundreds of the corporations' employees to do volunteer work. Marriott Hotels was the first corporation to answer this request, quickly followed by all the major banks, Coca-Cola, United Parcel Service, IBM, Southern Company, Georgia-Pacific, Home Depot, and ten others that were locally oriented. After a year or so, we expanded this idea to include a college or university to join the corporation as partner with each cluster.

The preeminent civil leader in Atlanta was Dan Sweat, who had assumed the role of overall TAP coordinator. Early in 1992, he and I went to Washington and met with President George H. W. Bush and his key cabinet members responsible for domestic programs. We outlined our findings and then shared them with a large assembly of House and Senate members. We had a long list of requests, including a special waiver of government application forms (we reduced the sixty-four pages to eight) and formation of a multiagency organization to serve Atlanta encompassing housing, welfare, health, employment, education, and the control of drugs and other crimes. With the help of Senator Sam Nunn, Congressman Newt Gingrich, and others, we were remarkably successful in this effort, as something of an experiment in domestic affairs.

We leased, without cost, a vacant floor of City Hall–East, the huge Sears, Roebuck building that had formerly served a seven-state area in filling mail orders from the Sears catalog. This gave us room for our growing organization. As the months went by, there were hundreds of exciting success stories and almost universal approbation and gratitude from the corporate and higher education partners.

The local population soon developed a new spirit, as community organizations were formed. They learned from one another and became increasingly vocal and persistent in their demands. We had a few difficult and sometimes embarrassing days as clusters laid out very ambitious prerequisites before they would accept their assigned corporations (including Coca-Cola Company) as partners, and I had to serve as a mediator on a few occasions. We all learned from one another as good innovations were highly publicized and shared.

Some of the banks formed three-hour training programs each Saturday morning to teach adults how to manage checking accounts and, after a subsequent test period, the participants could have their welfare payments mailed directly to the bank and write personal checks as needed. They could then avoid the high fees charged by moneylenders, eliminate the danger of having their government checks stolen, and shop where prices were lower. At the same time, banks obtained both new customers (often more dependable and careful than others) and good publicity for providing better services. Several dozen of the trained homeowners were hired to work full- or part-time in the banks. In addition, a reserve fund of about $12 million was established to make small business loans to TAP residents, with more than sixty loans made the first year.

All law enforcement organizations agreed to work as a team in the TAP area, which was a notable achievement in itself. This included eight city and county police forces, Georgia State Patrol, the state Bureau of Investigation, federal and state drug enforcement agencies, and even representatives of the various prison systems and probation officers. After the first couple of meetings, the group really seemed to enjoy this unprecedented chance to share experiences and opportunities. One practical innovation was to create a hotline that family members could use to report drug dealers, with full assurance of their identity being protected and of not having to appear in court. Within the large housing projects, some of the police patrols chose to ride bicycles in order to be more easily approached by homeowners.

To address the lack of immunization, we set aside one weekend to cover all twenty communities. Nearly twelve thousand volunteers visited every occupied home and recorded the status of health coverage for the children. Our primary incentive was a performance by Michael Jackson, who volunteered to give a concert with free tickets going to each family who proved with health department certificates that all its children had been immunized. This project revealed a lack of reliable records, and the state and local information was standardized and kept on computers instead of on file cards. This system was later expanded to include all of Georgia, and an attractive "youth passport" was developed to be issued to each of the 110,000 children born in the state each year, which would include a photograph, fingerprints, basic health instructions, and complete immunization records.

As a general policy, we encouraged each community to form six committees, to deal with economic development, criminal justice, community improvement, social services, housing, and health. Almost universally, the citizens abbreviated these to more descriptive names, such as jobs, safety, streets, schools, homes, and health.

We realized that the problems of drugs, school dropouts, teen pregnancy, and juvenile crime all related to young people, so, in partnership with the existing Cities in Schools program, we established the Future Force. This group ultimately comprised two thousand high school and middle school leaders of the future, and top priority in recruitment was given to those who had had some kind of trouble but were determined to improve their lives. These students were taken to the Fort Benning paratrooper school and to Georgia mountain camps for leadership training, and twenty of them were selected each winter to join Rosalynn and me (and about three hundred Carter Center donors) for a ski weekend at Crested Butte, Colorado. For most of them, this was their first airplane ride or involvement with snow. While there, the students maintained their schoolwork, wrote and performed an original play, mingled with our other guests, rode in dogsleds and snowmobiles, and learned to ski.

Some of them were fearless on the slopes. One night, after we had been at the lodge for just one full day, the ski patrol and instructors put on an exhibition for us by coming down the mountainside in single file, holding torches. In the distance, we noticed some wavering and even some interruptions in the beautiful procession, and when the skiers reached us, we were amazed to find that four of them were members of our Future Force! Three days later, two of the young men (former gang leaders in Atlanta) challenged each other to a race down the giant slalom course. The Future Force students were always an inspiration to the other participants in our Winter Weekend events, and we continued taking groups of them to these annual events long after the Atlanta Project was terminated.

There was intense news coverage, in both local and national media, and Dan Sweat and I spent an increasing amount of time giving interviews and making speeches in other large communities. We were surprised but gratified that this exposure created another serious problem for us. We were almost overwhelmed by delegations, sometimes including chartered planeloads of people, who came to Atlanta to learn what we were doing.

We finally decided to form a new organization, which we named The America Project, and hired a full-time staff to give briefings and inspection tours and to produce video descriptions and instruction pamphlets that other communities could use to create similar organizations. We shared this information and advice with more than four hundred other American cities and about a dozen delegations from other countries. I was even invited to go to London, where I gave a presentation to an assembly of civic and national leaders, including Crown Prince

Charles and three former prime ministers.

Our original plan was for The Atlanta Project to last for five years, from 1991 to 1996. We established criteria for each cluster community to meet, as judged by our staff, the corporate and university partners, and primarily the citizens involved. I had devoted an unanticipated portion of my own time and energy to this special work while trying not to neglect our international projects. During the final year, it was determined that six of the twenty communities were not ready to "graduate," so we extended those efforts for an additional three years, at a reduced annual cost of about $1.8 million. During this time we changed our overall goals to concentrate on four priorities: immunizing children by age two, increasing participation in preschool programs, minimizing dropouts from high school, and reducing second-child births among teenage mothers. We also eliminated the artificial boundaries that had separated the twenty cluster communities and moved most basic services from the large City Hall–East to four regional centers, nearer to families where need was greatest. At the end of that time, in 1999, we transferred responsibility (and remaining funds) to Georgia State University.

It is difficult to quantify the results of The

Atlanta Project, but we accomplished our original goals, which were (a) to identify the people in the metro Atlanta area who were most deserving of special attention, (b) to ensure that these families were given new hope and an opportunity to make decisions about their own future, and (c) to break down the barriers that existed between them and the relatively powerful and affluent leaders of our society. Our own ambitions grew as the months went by, and there is little doubt that some of the high expectations that evolved among the poor families were not realized. It was not always easy for us to accept facts and opinions in the cluster communities that conflicted with the long-held presumptions of us more affluent citizens. But hundreds of new leaders emerged, many of our joint achievements became permanent, and we saw some of our key proposals accepted by the state and federal governments.

Perhaps our wisest and most effective decision was the formation of partnerships within and between the cluster neighborhoods, and between them and major corporations and universities. This was a slow and evolutionary process, but there was a strong sense of sharing both a common future and mutual benefits. Atlanta has continued to benefit from closer ties among its own citizens and with hundreds of other American cities that have joined us in this effort. Of all the projects of The Carter Center, this has been one of the most difficult, challenging, exciting, and gratifying.

COUNCIL OF LEADERS

Robert Pastor had been my national security adviser for Latin America in the White House, where he helped to coordinate our successful effort to adopt the revised Panama Canal treaties. He was also responsible for the creation of the Hubert Humphrey Fellowship Program, which I announced in 1978. Through that program, more than 3,500 accomplished midlevel professionals from 140 countries have been brought to American universities for advanced study.

Pastor's first move as The Carter Center's Latin American fellow was to organize a consultation to analyze the impact of external debt on poorer nations, and another forum to strengthen democracy. This was an extension of our efforts while I was president to use the basic principles of human rights and freedom to replace the many Latin American military dictatorships with governments chosen by citizens in free and honest elections. During the second consultation, we greatly expanded the scope of

The Carter Center by organizing a group of political leaders from the Americas to serve as members of a Council of Freely Elected Heads of Government.

The original group included a dozen former presidents and prime ministers, and I agreed to serve as chairman, with Pastor as executive secretary. The most appropriate members, depending on their influence or language capabilities, could either join me or go on their own to deal with potential crises involving human rights abuses, dispute mediation, hyperinflation, contested titles to land following a revolution, or — most commonly — the monitoring of elections. The group was expanded to include sitting presidents, but more recently we decided to limit membership to leaders who are no longer in office, and the thirty-five-member council has continued to work throughout this hemisphere.

INTERNS

The Carter Center was very eager to expand our relationship with Emory to include other universities and, at the same time, we needed additional support for our small permanent staff. Having enjoyed the benefits of interns as governor and president, I naturally wanted to establish a similar program at our

Center. We decided that every intern would have a substantive work experience, and we have strictly enforced a policy ensuring that less than 30 percent of their role is focused on administrative tasks. Thus, interns play an integral part in our regular programmatic and operational activities. They work side by side with full-time staff members in promoting peace, monitoring elections, eradicating disease, enhancing mental health, and the other projects that our Center has undertaken.

Because of our high requirements for acceptance and the substantive nature of the interns' duties, *The Princeton Review* has always rated our program as "one of America's best."

Rosalynn and I are especially proud of the program, and we meet every class, give them a definitive briefing, answer their questions, and enjoy personal photographs with each intern. We are always impressed by the diversity of their backgrounds, their language skills, and their innovative spirit. We now average about a hundred interns each year, and have had over 2,000 who have come to us from almost 350 different universities and 57 nations. A class of thirty-five will usually speak a dozen languages fluently, and some of them have spent several years in the nations where our projects are focused.

In addition to their normal duties, members of each class of Carter Center interns are invited to spend a weekend with us in Plains, where they are able to better understand our formative years and get a glimpse of life in a small South Georgia community.

CHAPTER SIX
THE NEXT
TWENTY-FIVE YEARS

It is as difficult to predict the future of The Carter Center as it would have been in 1982 to envision the Center of today, but I am confident of our ability to accommodate change. We remember the steady and surprising progress we have made despite early shortages of funds, widely varying compatibility with different political leaders in Washington, unexpected trends in warfare, increasing commitments to democracy and health, and growing awareness of human suffering. We have a proven ability to take advantage of unforeseen challenges.

Now, with an adequate endowment, a strong and harmonious relationship with Emory University, and proven ties with other individuals and organizations, The Carter Center has a solid foundation for continuing its work after Rosalynn and I "reduce the level of our participation." Ably led by chairman John Moores, the members of our joint

Emory–Carter Center board of trustees have already increased their personal involvement and will shape all policies in the future. Some of their challenges and opportunities will evolve from our past experiences.

Emory University president James Wagner has continued the close relationship with The Carter Center first established by Jim Laney. Dr. John Hardman, president and CEO, directs a superb staff that implements the Center's multiple programs around the world.

One of our most sensitive relationships has been with the administrations of my successors in the White House. As a former president, I understand how unofficial intercessions could interfere in the implementation of official policy, and although tempted to break it on several occasions, we have maintained a policy of obtaining at least tacit approval from Washington before entering a sensitive political arena.

Primarily problems have resulted from our involvement with political leaders with whom the United States was refusing to communicate. As indicated in some of the earlier chapters, our controversial contacts have been with Mengistu Haile Mariam of Ethiopia, Mobutu Sese Seko of Zaire, Hafiz al-Assad of Syria, Raoul Cédras and Emile

Jonassaint of Haiti, Kim Il Sung of North Korea, Fidel Castro of Cuba, the Sandinistas of Nicaragua, some of the Palestinians, and the Bosnian Serbs. There will continue to be similar opportunities to go directly to the source of a problem or talk to the only person who might resolve a crisis. It may be easier for American political leaders to approve such intercessions by future leaders of The Carter Center who do not have a former president's high profile.

Our Center has never become directly involved in our nation's military affairs, but we recognize that the United States now has a defense budget that equals the sum total of all other nations' and is six times the second largest, in Russia. We have joined leaders of nuclear powers and others in attempts to alleviate the threat of a nuclear war and continue efforts to enforce and strengthen the Nuclear Non-Proliferation Treaty. With Washington now in the process of violating all extant treaty restraints on nuclear arsenals, it may be important for our Center to continue to address this subject.

American presidents have intervened more than a hundred times in foreign countries since I left office, in most cases using military force unnecessarily. The Carter Center must always stay alert for every opportunity

Togo, 2001 (Emily Staub)

to prevent or end deadly conflict. With our benevolent programs existing in some of the world's most troubled nations, we can be in the forefront of detecting these threats at an early stage. My hope is that we will enhance our ability to monitor the worldwide situation, to detect early threats to peace, and to move aggressively when non-governmental involvement is appropriate.

A good example is our special knowledge of the complex interrelationships in the Middle East and a proven willingness to remain directly involved despite the sensitive political restraints. Working closely with other organizations that espouse peace, justice, and respect for human rights, our Center must pursue every opportunity to realize these ideals for the people of Israel, the Palestinians, and others in the area.

I have expressed strong opposition to the recent adoption of preemptive war as a policy that departs radically from that of previous administrations. Within the bounds of political propriety, our Center can continue to cooperate with other responsible organizations that work to restore the United States' historical commitment to war as a last resort, avoiding destructive military action unless our national security is directly threatened.

The promotion of human rights has always covered the multiple and changing list of our current projects. We had assumed in earlier years that our own commitments and activities in support of human rights were in harmony with those of our government, and we were able to cooperate with officials in Washington. That is no longer a dependable premise. The Carter Center must stay in the forefront of efforts to implement all the commitments made almost sixty years ago in the Universal Declaration of Human Rights.

The Carter Center should continue to join other groups that focus on freedom and democracy, both in other nations and in our own. I have been active in promoting election reforms here at home, by working with President Gerald Ford after the 2000 debacle and with former secretary of state James Baker following the 2004 election. Much work remains to be done. If similar opportunities arise in the future, we should be willing to share our advice, derived from our many election experiences overseas.

One of my biggest surprises during the past quarter century has been the ever-increasing commitment of The Carter Center to preventing and eradicating tropical diseases. We have approached this expansion cau-

Palestine, 2005 (Thomas S. England)

tiously but with courage, and should continue to do so. Although we have recently become involved with the control of malaria, it is quite likely that our primary focus will continue to be on "neglected diseases," perhaps expanding our direct interest to dengue fever, leishmaniasis, or other afflictions as recommended by our International Task Force for Disease Eradication. We should also continue to work with others who are committed to increasing dramatically the level of humanitarian assistance from rich nations to people in desperate need.

One of the prime facets of our Global 2000 agriculture program in Africa has been enhancement of the environment through ending the traditional policy of slash and burn and preventing wind and water erosion of arable land. On a more generic basis, we participated fully in the planning session for the Kyoto Protocol, which evolved proposals adopted by most nations to deter global warming. This is likely to become even more pressing as a major issue to be addressed by The Carter Center.

Our eight-year commitment to The Atlanta Project was informative to us and gratifying to the deprived families in our own community. As described in Chapter 5, some seminal laws and regulations of the federal and state governments and administrative policies of corporations were changed. Almost four hundred other American communities also learned about how to form beneficial relationships between poor people, their governments, wealthier neighbors, business and financial institutions, and nearby colleges and universities. Since benefits tend to dissipate over time, this is an area of opportunity that might well be visited again.

The crucial factors that will determine the viability of The Carter Center are an innovative spirit, an insistence on complete independence, and a dedicated and competent staff. We must continue to probe for every opportunity to fill vacuums of need in the world and have the courage to take a chance on possible failure if the goal is worthy. There is no alternative to our sustained status as an institution that considers the most difficult and important issues without timidity and then takes bold action without restraint. It has always been helpful to reach out to other organizations that share our goals and to form constructive partnerships without concern about who receives credit for successes.

We take heart from worldwide trends toward democracy. According to Freedom House, only 84 independent nations were

Indonesia, 1999 (YURIAH TANZIL)

free or partly free when I became president in 1977. Now this number has increased to 149. One of our top priorities will be to help this trend continue. As a nongovernmental organization, our Center has the advantage of being able to go anywhere the emergence of a new democracy is possible or to help preserve one that is endangered. These same opportunities exist where there are real threats of deadly conflict.

Our health programs deal with physical ailments and peace programs with political ills. The science and technology of the former is much more advanced, but we consider both these areas to be closely related, and The Carter Center has been able to deal with them both. Sustaining and deepening this dual commitment will be an exciting and gratifying challenge.

In general, the principles of The Carter Center have been the same ones that should characterize our nation, or any individual. They are the beliefs inherent in all the great world religions, including commitments to peace, justice, freedom, humility, forgiveness or an attempt to find accommodation with potential foes, generosity, human rights or fair treatment of others, protection of the environment, and the alleviation of suffering. This is our agenda for the future.

Rosalynn and I devote almost all our time and effort to the work of The Carter Center, but we spend a week each year as volunteers for Habitat for Humanity. Beginning in 1984, we have recruited others to join us in building homes for poor families in need. In the early years we concentrated almost exclusively on the poorest areas of major U.S. cities, including New York, Chicago, Philadelphia, Atlanta, Los Angeles, Houston, and Milwaukee. We then began alternating between foreign nations and America.

We work alongside adults from the homeowner families, chosen by local Habitat councils who are familiar with the area. The homes are modest in size but comfortable, and the designs are compatible with surrounding architecture. The families must pay full price for their homes, but we follow the biblical admonition against charging interest to poor people. Usually with twenty-year mortgages, the monthly payments can be made by those with limited income.

Family members are required to contribute about five hundred hours of "sweat equity," and usually help to prepare the building site and the house foundation before we arrive. Then they work with us for the five days required to complete the homes. We frame most of our American houses with lumber, but concrete blocks are more common in foreign countries.

The number of volunteers per house depends on its size. Habitat can complete small homes (30 square meters) with twelve workers. About thirty-five workers are required for our larger homes, which are about four times as large. Our custom is to arrive on the building site Sunday afternoon, have a conference to explain all the safety rules and procedures that night, then begin erecting walls early Monday. Our goal is to complete the construction on Friday, with the site landscaped and stoves, refrigerators, and other necessary furnishings installed. There are almost always many tears shed during brief ceremonies when we hand the keys to the homeowners, along with a Bible when appropriate.

Rosalynn and I, with members of our family and thousands of volunteers, have enjoyed our projects in Mexico (three cities), Canada, the Philippines, Hungary, South Africa, South Korea, and India. Our largest project was in five communities in the Philippines, with 293 homes completed. We had more than ten thousand others join us, including those who provided food and health services or kept us masons supplied with mortar mix and other supplies. We try to limit foreigners to no more than one-half the total of workers so that homeowner families and their fellow citizens have a chance to participate.

Habitat for Humanity is an exciting complement to our work at The Carter Center.

ACKNOWLEDGMENTS

The evolution of this book has been a partnership between me and many others who are instrumental in achieving the successes of The Carter Center. As the author, I am especially grateful to my assistant, *Lauren Gay,* who has helped to coordinate the entire project. *Deanna Congileo* has worked closely with me and Simon & Schuster to organize the text, the photographs, and the insertion of vignettes. *Dr. Steve Hochman,* my special assistant since the Center was conceived, has been the primary monitor of historical accuracy. *Phillip Wise,* in charge of operations at The Carter Center, was my White House appointments secretary and has been responsible for our successful fund-raising efforts; he also monitors the proper expenditure of these funds.

With only a portion of their crucial roles described in the text, there are a number of leaders who deserve additional mention.

Dr. John Hardman, as president and CEO of The Carter Center, provides leadership to achieve the Center's commitment to advance peace, health, and human rights worldwide. *Dr. Donald R. Hopkins* is vice president for health programs. Before this job, he led the Center's effort to eradicate Guinea worm disease and to help control river blindness worldwide. *Dr. John Stremlau* is vice president in charge of all our peace programs. *Dr. Thomas H. Bornemann,* who directs the Center's Mental Health Program, has worked in all aspects of public mental health care, including clinical practice, research, management, policy development, and administration at the national level. *Dr. Jennifer McCoy* is in charge of the Center's Americas Program and is a political science professor at Georgia State University. *Dr. Frank Richards* coordinates the river blindness, schistosomiasis, and lymphatic filariasis control programs and the malaria control initiative. *Dr. Yawei Liu* directs the China Program, an unprecedented partnership with the Chinese government to standardize village election practices. *Dr. David Carroll,* director of the Center's Democracy Program, has managed more than twenty Carter Center election observation missions. *Karin Ryan* directs the Human Rights Program, including efforts on behalf of victims of human rights violations and human rights defenders. *Dr. Norman Borlaug,* a Nobel Peace laureate, leads the Sasakawa–Global 2000 Agriculture Program, a joint venture between the Sasakawa Africa Association and The Carter Center. *Dr. Bill Foege,* fellow for health policy at The Carter Center, was executive director of the Center from 1986 to 1992. He directed the campaign to eradicate smallpox in the 1970s. *Dr. Ernesto Ruiz-Tiben* is in charge of the Guinea Worm Eradication Program. *Dr. Paul Emerson,* who directs the Trachoma Control Program, has spent nearly a decade devoted to operational research and program evaluation in support of the global effort to control trachoma. *Craig Withers,* director of health program support, manages international development activities in health and food security in nineteen African and Latin American countries. *Dr. Joyce P. Murray,* professor of nursing at the Nell Hodgson Woodruff School of Nursing at Emory University, directs the Ethiopia Public Health Training Initiative, a teacher training program enabling Ethiopia to meet staffing needs for more than five hundred community health centers nationwide.

My editor, *Alice Mayhew,* has continued a delightful and productive partnership between me and Simon & Schuster, ably assisted by *Serena Jones* and production editor *Mara Lurie.* Also, I am grateful for my longtime friend and agent *Lynn Nesbit.*

ABOUT THE AUTHOR

Jimmy Carter was born in Plains, Georgia, and served as thirty-ninth President of the United States. He and his wife, Rosalynn, founded The Carter Center, a nonprofit organization that prevents and resolves conflicts, enhances freedom and democracy, and improves health around the world. He is the author of numerous books, including *An Hour Before Daylight,* called "an American classic," and the #1 *New York Times* bestseller *Our Endangered Values.* Since leaving the presidency in 1981, President Carter has earned a Nobel Peace Prize for his humanitarian work at The Carter Center.